DIVORCE IN MISSOURI

By Missouri Attorneys
Alan Freed
Alisse Camazine

with
John Pavese

ACORN HOUSE
Book Publishers
Hertford, North Carolina

Composition by Beckwith Bookworks.
Cover design by Hannus Design.
Cover art by Dave Sullivan.

Library of Congress Catalog Card Number: 2008940193

_____

ISBN 978-09745101-2-5

Printed in the United States of America

Publishing History
9 8 7 6 5 4 3 2 1

Acorn House
123 Pigeon River Court, Hertford, North Carolina 27944
www.divorceinmo.com

Contents

To the memory of Howard Freed, who demonstrated the beauty of marriage through almost 63 years of dedication to his loving bride, Betty.

Acknowledgments

The authors wish to thank the following individuals for their help in completing *Divorce in Missouri*.

Gary Waint, Director of Juvenile and Adult Court Programs; Office of State Courts Administrator Kathleen Bird of the Family Court, 7th Judicial Circuit; Peter Schloss, Larry Swall, Joanne Dyroff and our other colleagues at Paule, Camazine & Blumenthal; and, of course, our families for their patience in allowing us the time to complete this labor of love.

Introduction

This is not a touchy-feely book. It will not hold your hand and shed sympathetic tears. It certainly doesn't provide marriage counseling. Most important, it has no method or desire to prove that your spouse is a reprobate. Any therapeutic value comes from the comfort of finally understanding the divorce process.

The sooner you focus on the future and not the past the better for everyone, especially for you! The only ones who get rich from vengeance and spite are the lawyers. Missouri judges who sense it's all about revenge have no time for the individuals who revel in it or for their attorneys.

Each state has its individual laws regarding divorce. Even when the laws are similar, how state courts apply and interpret those laws can be quite different. However, books on divorce typically fail to explain these differences.

Divorce in Missouri focuses only on Missouri. It explains the important issues you need to understand in order to make informed decisions. Make no mistake; this is a complicated procedure. So as you move through the divorce process, refer back to this book to regain your bearings and prepare both emotionally and logistically for the next steps.

Ironically, you will find that the same virtues that work to make a marriage successful are necessary to have a satisfactory divorce. Indeed, if both parties approach the divorce process with realistic expectations, a desire to understand their partner's point of view, and a willingness to play fair, there's a good chance that a "livable" result can be reached without great pain.

However, if one or both of the players view the divorce as a vehicle for inflicting punishment or for gaining financially or emotionally at the expense of the other side, then be prepared for a rough trip. In such cases there are no winners and losers, but only losers.

Now you're thinking, "That so and so who has made my marriage so miserable is going to make my divorce miserable too! How are we ever going to reach a peaceful agreement?"

Well for one thing, consider that you both have a lot more at stake in a divorce than in a marriage. In a marriage there is only the *potential* for disaster. In divorce disaster is a near-term reality. So both sides had better "get real" and quickly.

Use this book, also, to decide if you will be better off after divorce. Don't jump to the conclusion that divorce is the only answer. When children are involved, both parents will likely see them less after the divorce than before. Perhaps quite a bit less.

And then there are the financial obligations. Those commitments usually get worse following a divorce because there are now two separate households to support on essentially the same income. Remember that a major cause of poverty in the U.S. today is DIVORCE!

Sure your spouse drives you crazy, but marriage is only one of the ways to be miserable. Consider the fun of moving in with your parents because there is no decent place in Springfield that you can afford to rent for your "bachelor pad." Or the equally pleasant experience of managing the house and kids all on your own while having to go out and get a full time job because the Missouri court says you should be working. And all the time raising the children on an orchestrated visitation schedule.

Finally, understand that whatever you decide to do, you will not be alone. There are well over 20,000 divorces in Missouri every year. Half of all marriages in the U.S. end in divorce. And for recent marriages the divorce figure is even higher.

No doubt a lot more people consider divorce and decide not to proceed. Either way it's a decision only you can make. Only you know what you will be in for if your marriage continues. *Divorce in Missouri* shows what the way out looks like.

Authors' Note

A System Full of Humans

The problem with any legal system is that it is written by, used by, and administered by . . . human beings. That is as true in Missouri as it is anywhere else.

Replace the judges and lawyers with computers, make every spouse's needs, finances, and abilities the same, and things become much simpler to plan and predict. But we all know nothing in life is that way. For sure divorce isn't like that.

The system doesn't work so it is done 80% of the time this way and 20% of the time this other way. More likely it is done 80% one way and 2% another way and 6% another way and 4% another way, etc., until you make up that other 20%.

This makes it hard to write a book giving specific information on a topic that is so variable. The only way to do it is to focus on what is usually the case. Trying to list all the alternative possibilities is an endless task. Everyone would find it just too confusing.

The Most Good for the Most People

So your situation may not always fit exactly into the examples and likely results given. This doesn't mean the book is wrong. It just means you are an exception.

When you see words like "usually" or "frequently" or "sometimes" or "often" before a statement, your antennae should go up. We mean to say that it isn't "always" the case. Rather, it's only "frequently" or "usually" the case, or whatever. If such a comment deals with a critical part of your divorce, it's a good issue to review with a lawyer.

That being said, everyone reading this book will come away knowing a lot more about his or her divorce. No matter what your situation, a good portion of it will fit into the book's discussion.

Lawyers, God Bless Them ... and Judges Too!
Part of the problem is that the law doesn't stand still. Attorneys are always out there trying to change the interpretation of the law. Hey, that's what you pay them to do. Does anyone want their lawyer to send them into a meat grinder when there may be a way around it?

Judges, who are human as well, just add to the mix. We try to give you a likely outcome, but when it gets down to a certain judge on a certain day, well, nothing is certain. Anyway, the end result is that it all becomes kind of a moving target.

A Fairly Fair Process
Therefore, any couple relying on a judge to decide the final terms of their divorce is taking the chance that the court will decide more favorably for the other side. The intention of the law is to treat everyone equally. However, "equally" isn't a clearly defined legal term in Missouri. What is equal to one judge may be different in the eyes of another.

This is especially true when it comes to awarding the physical custody of a child and to determining spousal support (alimony). There are still some judges, particularly in rural areas, who have a traditional (you might call it old-fashioned) view of women and men in the family.

They feel that women are inherently the primary caregivers and men are meant to be the primary providers. This viewpoint has resulted in decisions that by modern standards don't appear to be evenhanded. Yet, they are rarely overturned if appealed.

Attitudes are changing, but it's a slow process. Men seeking a divorce today must recognize this reality. They may have greater downside risk regarding these two areas (physical custody and maintenance) than do women. So it's often better for a man to make every effort to settle these matters before a trial than to roll the dice in court.

At the same time, this shouldn't encourage women to drag things into court if it can be avoided. There's more to a divorce than just these two items, and predicting how the judge will decide on all the issues is just not possible.

Some Poetic License Taken

Each chapter gives examples of cases that demonstrate whatever point is trying to be made at the time. While these cases represent realistic situations, they do not refer to actual circumstances. In other words, it's the usual "any similarity to persons and events living or dead is just a coincidence."

How to Act in Court

Many of the procedures in the Circuit Court where your divorce will be tried are based on practices dating back hundreds of years. Some important ones are quite subtle and not necessarily covered in this book. The good intentions of people representing themselves are not always enough. Failure to understand courtroom etiquette can negatively affect how the judge views you and your point of view. Lawyers are trained to ensure this doesn't happen.

However, we know that many readers will be in court without a lawyer. That's your right. It's also your responsibility to prepare yourself for this experience. Don't underestimate the importance of knowing the do's and don't's of courtroom manners and protocol. Seek advice from those who are familiar with the process.

The Price You're Going to Pay
The fees and average charges mentioned in this book were current at the time of publication. However, we all are painfully aware that from gasoline to prescription medicines, as well as for everything in between, prices are on the rise. So it's quite possible that the costs we list may be different from those you experience. Sorry!

Do Not Remove This Page
Under Penalty of Law
If everything mentioned so far looks a lot like a legal disclaimer, that's because it is.

We hope to provide a sense of direction regarding the divorce process and to make the reader sensitive to possibilities and consequences of which he or she may not be aware. Hopefully, this will reduce the surprises and save some aggravation and money. Of course, the main goal is to reach a sound settlement.

But the legal environment is constantly changing. We strongly suggest consulting with a lawyer. A personal

attorney is in the best position to understand the impli-
cations of your specific situation.

Can you do a divorce successfully without a lawyer?
Under the right conditions, absolutely. But you'll need
more information than is contained in this book. Seek the
help of mediators, counselors, and state agencies. Many
services are available at reduced cost for low income
families.

This book will teach you a lot, but learning where the
udder is doesn't necessarily mean you know how to milk
the cow.

CHAPTER 1

Grounds for Divorce

A Quick History Lesson

BESIDES LAYING OUT Missouri's divorce process, this book provides some perspective on both the court system and the laws it administers. Knowing a little bit about how things evolved will hopefully increase your comfort level.

A long time ago when Missouri was completely unexplored and most of Europe was of the Catholic faith, all divorces in that part of the world had to be approved by the Pope. One day King Henry VIII of England requested a divorce, but the Pope wouldn't agree. Kings don't like to be denied, so Henry created the Church of England. Freed from having to please the Pope, Henry promptly got his divorce.

Thus divorce began its movement away from being dominated by strict religious doctrine. (Apologies to the Catholic church, the Church of England, and England in general for this abbreviated and probably somewhat inaccurate moment in history.)

By the time the U.S. became a fledgling nation the concept of divorce was even more advanced. It had become
largely a legal issue with fewer religious overtones.
Missouri, like the other states, established a number of
grounds based upon which a spouse could seek a
divorce (adultery, abuse, abandonment, etc.).

For sure, the courts were not eager to grant a divorce just
because someone wanted one. Splitting up a family in
the 1800s and early 1900s raised even greater financial
concerns than it does today. What would happen to the
divorced women and their children? (There weren't too
many female corporate vice presidents in those days.)

Since then, and particularly since World War II, the situation has changed dramatically. Women started to get
jobs that allowed them to live independently. Some
could even afford to raise a family as a single parent.
Unfortunately, divorce laws were slow to adjust to this
emerging "new world." There was still no simple way to
dissolve a marriage.

Missourians with money could hop a plane to Mexico,
the Dominican Republic, or Haiti for a quickie divorce.
Lawyers liked this approach as long as they got invited
along to make sure that it all went smoothly. January and
February were particularly attractive months for a tropi-
cal split.

But most couples in the Show-Me State had to find a less
expensive method to end things. In situations where
both sides wanted the divorce, one of the partners would
often admit to having committed some divorceable fault,
while the other partner played along. Sympathetic
judges turned a blind eye to the game and granted the
divorce.

This all changed in the 1970s when Missouri's legislature simplified the divorce process. Finally, an individual could end a marriage simply because it was what he or she wanted. The only requirement was to show that the marriage was broken and there was no hope of it being fixed. No one had to be at fault.

One-Way Exit

Nevertheless, many people believe that Missouri has several grounds for dissolving a marriage. Adultery and abuse are often the likely suspects, with abandonment or desertion not far behind. That's just not true.

Missouri is a "no-fault" state and there's only one ground for getting a divorce. The court simply needs to conclude that the marriage can't be made to work—that the union is "irretrievably broken and there is no reasonable likelihood that the marriage can be preserved." Finding out who did what to whom is not always so important. Objectionable behavior (adultery, etc.) might be used as evidence to reach this conclusion, but usually it's not.

When both sides agree that the marriage is irretrievably broken and have settled all the issues of divorce (children, support, property, etc.), the procedure is often quite fast moving. Judgments in as little as 45 to 60 days are possible. Welcome to the world of no-fault divorce.

Dealing with an Objecting Party

Unfortunately, things don't always go so smoothly. Whether or not a couple should get divorced sometimes turns into just another argument. One side seeks to end things while the other wants to "stay the course." Under these circumstances the court is required to further explore the matter.

Missouri law stipulates that if one party denies under oath that the marriage is broken, the petitioner (the person filing for divorce) must demonstrate one or more of the following:

1. The other party committed adultery.

2. The other party behaved in such a way that the petitioner cannot be expected to live with that party.

3. The other party abandoned the petitioner for at least six months preceding the divorce filing.

4. The parties lived apart by mutual consent for at least one year preceding the divorce filing.

5. The parties lived separate and apart for at least two years (no mutual consent) preceding the divorce filing.

But don't be misled into thinking that a spouse who doesn't want the divorce can triumphantly argue in court that none of the above five items has occurred. Actually, it's a rare case when any of these issues gets raised.

Basically, if one party testifies that the marriage is broken and cannot be repaired, the dissolution (the divorce) will be granted. Forget about any argument raised by the other spouse.

The Conduct of the Parties

So does that mean the conduct of the parties during the marriage doesn't matter? Not necessarily.

If one of the parties frequently abused the other or was

involved in serious criminal activity or was continually unfaithful, it's worth mentioning such bad behavior to the court. The "conduct of the parties" is one of several items considered by the court when determining the final judgment.

Should you end up in a trial (instead of a negotiated settlement), your lawyer can raise the issues of adultery, etc., and provide the necessary proof at the time the maintenance (alimony) and property awards are being decided. If the situation was bad enough the injured spouse will sometimes receive more favorable treatment in these areas (refer to the maintenance and property chapters).

But don't get too excited either way. Many other issues also influence how maintenance and the assets will be handed out. Things like adultery are usually not the most important factors.

In addition, the degree that poor conduct will enter into the deliberation is likely to vary depending on the part of the state where the divorce takes place. There's no hard-and-fast formula that a judge must apply. A court in a conservative part of Missouri might see things a little differently from one in a more liberal area. That's one reason why going to trial instead of negotiating a settlement is always risky.

So while their use is limited, let's take a brief look at how the law defines these conduct issues. Just remember that their main function is to possibly influence the structure of the final judgment. Rarely are they used to prove the marriage has died, and never as grounds for divorce.

Spousal alert! Anything (adultery, drugs/alcohol, abuse, etc.) you ask your spouse to testify to either in a sworn document or at the trial will be under oath. And he or she has the right to ask you to testify to the exact same questions.

Adultery, Just One of Those Flings

The Show-Me State doesn't clearly define adultery. Commonly it's considered to be having sexual relations with a person other than one's spouse. Based on 1990s presidential history, that's still a bit vague, but you can be certain a Missouri court will know it when it sees it. Meanwhile, to get a definition of adultery that will work best for you, just ask your marriage partner. Once you know what adultery is, you have to prove that it happened. Surprisingly, the most popular method of doing this is by confession. Going the private detective route with the sordid testimony, photographs, etc., makes for interesting movies, but is this how you want to run your real life? After all, divorce trials and any photographic evidence are normally part of the public record.

Incompatibly Bad Behavior

Sometimes things aren't what you expected. People can quickly change after the wedding. Maybe one or the other spouse wasn't paying enough attention to personality details before the nuptials. Does that actually happen?

Compatibility issues may also develop over a longer period of time. Little things that once didn't seem to be important suddenly become so. Relationships can just wear out.

Then there are occasions when the behavior of a spouse is really disruptive, and living together is simply not an option. For example, in situations where there has been physical or mental abuse, criminal activity, drug/alcohol excesses, etc., the good spouse may find it impossible to remain married.

Living Apart and Abandonment

If you're going to contend that the marriage is broken based on the living apart or abandonment criteria listed above, it's important to keep a few things in mind.

The first is that the specified periods of separation (6, 12, and 24 months) must be consecutive—not two months in 2006 and four months in 2008, etc. Equally important is that the separation period must have occurred immediately prior to filing for divorce and still be continuing. For example, if you were abandoned for six months in a row but now are back together, that just won't work in Missouri.

Most couples accomplish the 12 months of mutually consensual separation by having one spouse move to a different address. However, some parties successfully demonstrate to the court that they lived separate lives for the entire period while sharing the same roof. (Didn't Sonny and Cher do that for a while? Or was it Bill and Hillary?) Anyway, that being said, it's often easier to get through the divorce process if individual residences are maintained.

OK, that makes sense, but why does the law make a distinction between being abandoned for six months and living apart without mutual consent for 24 months?

The difference is that under the law one party can live apart from the other without abandoning him or her. Abandonment means that the wayward spouse not only has left the home, but he or she also is no longer participating in the family. This includes failing to provide economic and other support to the left-behind spouse and the kids.

However, it's possible for a party to move down the road from the family home for six months or more while still interacting with the family. He or she can help pay the expenses, paint the house, drive the kids to the big game, and do most of the things expected of such a spouse before the move. The marriage may be finished, but clearly the family hasn't been abandoned.

Taking the High Ground

In summary, the most important benefit of the no-fault approach is that the focus shifts from placing the blame on someone to structuring the most beneficial deal for everyone (especially the kids) in life after the divorce.

Yes, if the two parties disagree on ending the marriage, the judge will take the time to listen to both sides and see if things can be saved. But don't expect the court to perform or require marriage counseling (something that should have been done much earlier). Indeed, the law specifically forbids it from doing so.

In the end no judge is going to force a couple to stay married if one side is looking to get out. The spouse wanting the divorce will always get his or her wish.

Compared to the days of divorces based on finding fault, the no-fault process is a tremendous improvement. This is true despite the fact that you won't find the term in any Missouri statue. That's because "no-fault divorce" isn't a legal term. Nevertheless, it's a pretty good system, especially considering our government is involved.

CHAPTER 2

Missouri's Divorce Process

We Know What We're Doing and Other Smart Comments

SOME OF THE INFORMATION included in this chapter also appears in other sections of the book. It's worth repeating. If you don't get a solid understanding of what's being decided at each step, and by whom, the process will be overwhelming.

Laying out the legal system in a single discussion (as in this chapter), combined with reminders of the process within chapters that discuss specific issues (e.g. child custody, child support, maintenance, etc.), will hopefully reinforce this understanding. After all, it's complicated. Law students get three years to figure it out. That's a lot more time than you have.

Read carefully. As St. Louis native Yogi Berra once said, "If you don't know where you're going, you'll wind up somewhere else."

A Language Lesson

Let's define some of the important terms you'll run across during the upcoming legal adventure. Even when using a lawyer, knowing this basic vocabulary should increase your comfort factor.

Remember, U.S. courts are based on old English law so naturally many of the terms used today also date back that far. They are fashioned after the way conversations were conducted between serfs and their feudal lords. Anyway, here are just a few to keep in mind.

Petition—A formal written request to a court for an order of the court, such as a request for a divorce.

Prayer—The specific request for a judgment, relief, or damages at the conclusion of a petition. In terms of a divorce, it could indicate what a person wants from the other spouse.

Answer—A written pleading filed by the person receiving a petition. It can deny or admit the issues in the petition or raise other issues.

Stipulation—An agreement between parties or by an individual party that a certain fact is true or uncontested. Also, an agreement by the parties to certain procedures or actions (such as who will have legal custody of a child) can be stipulated to the court. The important thing is that stipulations eliminate the need for the judge to decide an issue or a fact.

Hearing—A legal proceeding (other than a full-scale trial) held before a judge. During a hearing, arguments and sometimes evidence are presented. Hearings typically occur prior to a trial in order to have the judge resolve a specific issue.

Trial—A legal proceeding presided over by a judge at which evidence is presented by witnesses. The purpose is to examine the facts and law related to an issue (such as a divorce) and reach a binding decision.

Settlement versus judgment—A settlement is an agreement that a couple reaches out of court. Judges don't issue settlements; they issue judgments, orders, or decrees. If the couple in a divorce reaches a settlement, the judge is likely to issue a "final judgment" (also called a "final order" or "decree of dissolution") incorporating the couple's settlement.

Motion—Any formal request made to a judge for an order or judgment or to change an order or judgment. They are usually in writing and include the reasons why the motion should be granted. A motion seeking to change child support, child custody, or maintenance is referred to as a "motion to modify."

Getting the Lowdown on the Family Court

Divorce in the more populated parts of Missouri revolves around the Family Court. While the Family Court seems to have been around forever, it's actually a relatively new development. Up until the early 1990s, divorces were not separated from the rest of the matters that came before the Circuit Court.

This meant that judges were often doing divorces between trying murderers and hearing civil suits. While that made for an interesting day, it was hard for judges to stay at the top of their game in all the areas of the law. Yes, murder was more serious than divorce, but some argued that the scope and complexity of divorce issues were often greater than those found in criminal offenses. Regardless, they were definitely different.

Judges focused only on family law would certainly improve the quality of their work. Another benefit was that the Family Court would project a softer, less businesslike, style of justice, at least compared to courts handling criminal matters.

The end result was hoped to be a courtroom experience that, if not completely user friendly, at least did not add to the pain and conflict already being suffered by the Show-Me State citizens who ventured into it. And so in 1993, the Missouri legislature created the Family Court.

The Family Court not only handles cases related to separation and divorce (and modifications to both), it also takes on juvenile, paternity, and abuse issues.

So how have things worked out? Well, in some cases Family Court judges in smaller court districts have not been able to focus exclusively on family law. Other circuits assigned their most junior judges to the Family Court.

None of this is to say that the Family Court is a failure. It just hasn't achieved some of its loftier goals. In general, the quality of the court improved. And the "softer" feeling of the court did calm some people down.

Some Things Haven't Changed

While most Missourians get to use a Family Court for their divorce, not everyone can. Smaller circuits just don't have the customer volume to justify setting up a separate Family Court. In these situations having your divorce heard by a judge who just presided over a hit-and-run trial is not unusual.

It's not a perfect system, and something is certainly lost if a judge's scope is too broad. Nevertheless, the laws of the state are the same in all courtrooms. It's up to the judges to ensure that every citizen's rights get properly upheld.

Knowing Missouri's Court Structure

This is a good time to find out where the Family Court fits into Missouri's court structure.

The backbone of the entire system is the Circuit Court. There are 45 circuits across the state. In densely populated areas a circuit will cover only one county. The City of St. Louis alone is one circuit. In other parts of the state several counties may fall under one circuit. Regardless, there is a Circuit Court building in every county, usually in the county seat. Some counties have more than one. (To find out the location and telephone number of the Circuit Court in your county, go to www.courts.mo.gov or telephone the Office of State Courts Administrator at 573-751-4377.)

Each Circuit Court has several divisions. Depending on the size of the Circuit Court, it can be made up of some or all of the following: associate circuit, civil, small claims, municipal, probate, criminal, juvenile, and family. If there's a Family Court, that's where all the activities surrounding a divorce will occur. If the Circuit Court doesn't have a Family Court, then the divorce is conducted in the civil division of the Circuit Court.

The Missouri Court of Appeals reviews cases heard by the Circuit Courts. The three Court of Appeals districts are referred to as the Eastern, the Western, and the Southern. It is to one of these courts you will proceed (most often with a lawyer and checkbook in hand) if you decide to appeal a divorce judgment.

The Missouri Supreme Court is the highest court in the state. Should you ever reach this level during your cruise aboard the good ship *SS Divorce*, it has been for certain not a bon voyage. Enough said.

Circuit Judges, Associate Circuit Judges, and Sometimes Commissioners

In Missouri there are three options when it comes to who will judge your divorce. Throughout the book the term "judge" is used, but in fact it could be a circuit judge, an associate circuit judge, or a commissioner.

Circuit judges have reached the highest status in the Circuit Court. Below them, but equally important from the standpoint of your divorce, are associate circuit judges. Most of these judges are elected in Missouri, but in certain urban areas their appointment is made through a nonpartisan selection process. Nevertheless, they all must be periodically approved by the voters to remain in their positions.

Commissioners are generally found in the more metropolitan areas of the state. They are selected by the circuit judges and associate circuit judges for the relevant district. With a few exceptions, commissioners have the same qualifications and authority as the two judge types. However, commissioners are able to hear cases only in the Family Court.

From a practical standpoint it makes little difference which of the three possibilities is assigned your case.

Everything in Due Time

Justice sometimes moves slowly, but that doesn't mean there isn't a schedule. In fact, some Missouri courts are pretty spry with regard to getting divorce cases resolved.

Throughout this book there are references to the number of days by which something must be completed by either party or the court itself. In all cases this is a reference to the number of *calendar days* within which the action must take place. It's not the number of *business days*. For example, if something has to be completed within 30 days, that includes Saturdays, Sundays, and Missouri state holidays.

The exception is if the last day of the relevant period is a Saturday, Sunday, or Missouri state holiday. In that case the last day is moved to the next business day. So if the end of the required 30-day period is a Saturday, the final day becomes the following Monday. If the last day is the Fourth of July, then the final day is moved to the fifth unless the fifth is a Saturday or Sunday. In that case it's moved to the next Monday.

These time requirements are very important to the court. A judge usually isn't going to allow them to be ignored even by one extra day. So if you're uncertain about a due date, get clarification. If something must be mailed make sure you register it and keep the receipt.

And don't forget the dates when it comes to residency requirements. In order to file for a divorce in Missouri, at least one of the spouses has to have been a resident of the state for the most recent 90-day period. Once the divorce is properly filed, neither spouse is required to reside in the state.

However, there are restrictions about permanently taking the children out of state without the approval of either the other party or the court (discussed later in this chapter and also in the chapter on physical and legal custody).

It Starts with a Petition

Only a marriage partner can begin the divorce process. Divorce isn't a crime observed by a third party and reported to the police for prosecution. Criminal abuse of a child or spouse can be reported by anyone and, if proven to be true, the court (the Criminal Court, not the Family Court) will punish the guilty. But even under those circumstances a judge cannot order a divorce.

So if either spouse wants a divorce, he or she must be the one to get things rolling. If both want a divorce, they can flip a coin to decide who files. It makes no difference who initiates the filing.

Assuming the filing spouse has a lawyer, the first step will be for the attorney to draw up a divorce petition. If the party wanting to initiate the divorce has no lawyer (called going "*pro se*" and pronounced "pro say"), the first step is to get a petition form.

The easiest way to get one is by visiting www.courts.mo.gov. That's the Missouri court website. Click on "Representing Yourself" under the "Quick Links" section and it will take you to a lot of information on *pro se* activities, including a petition form.

Circuit clerks will be happy to provide some basic instructions on how to fill out the petition form (along with taking the filing fee). But they are barred by law from providing you with any legal advice. You're on your own.

The Anatomy of a Petition

The petition will specify the basis for seeking a divorce. In the old days, this frequently required accusing the other spouse of adultery or abuse or some other personality deficit. Today, virtually all the petitions simply state that the marriage is "irretrievably broken" and that there is "no reasonable likelihood that the marriage can be preserved." Rarely are specific acts of misconduct listed.

In addition to the divorce grounds, the petition includes a lot of family data. So if you have an appointment with a lawyer to initiate a petition, it makes sense to bring the following information to the meeting:

1. Names, addresses, and Social Security numbers of the spouses and how long each has lived in the county and the state.

2. Date of the marriage and where it is registered (state and county).

3. Date of the separation (when the couple stopped living as husband and wife).

4. Names, addresses, and Social Security numbers of all minor (under age 18) children.

5. Names, addresses, and Social Security numbers of all children 18 years old or older who are dependent due to physical or mental disabilities or are still in a qualifying education program (explained in the chapter on child support).

6. The parent each child has primarily lived with for the six months immediately prior to filing the petition. Include the details of any court intervention or guardianships. The petitioner must be able to state that with respect to the minor children, the petitioner:

   a. hasn't participated in any capacity in any other litigation concerning the custody of the minor children in Missouri or any other state;

   b. has no knowledge of any custody proceeding concerning the minor children pending in Missouri or any other state;

   c. knows of no other person not a party to the proceedings under this petition who has physical custody of the minor children or who claims to have custody or visitation rights.

7. Any arrangements regarding child custody and support as well as maintenance (alimony) that the spouses have agreed to even if it is only for a temporary basis.

8. Whether the wife is pregnant.

The petition is signed by the petitioning spouse under oath before a notary public.

Deciding Where to File

The spouse initiating the petition can choose to file it in either the county where he or she lives or in the county where the other spouse lives. However, if the petition is filed in the county where the petitioning spouse resides, the other spouse (referred to as the "respondent") can request that the court move the case to the respondent's county.

The court will go along with this requested change if

1. the respondent's county is where the children have resided during the 90 days immediately prior to the petition being filed; or

2. the move to the respondent's county is in the best interests of the kids because

   • the children and at least one parent have a strong connection with the county;

   • there is substantial evidence in the county (school teachers, doctor, scoutmaster, grandparents, etc.) concerning the present or future care, protection, and personal relationships of the children.

Sometimes, neither spouse wants to do the divorce in the county where they reside. Don't forget, divorces are open to the public without invitation. Anyway, if both sides agree, the court will allow the couple to "waive venue" and move the divorce to a county they prefer.

One last point about filing. If one spouse lives in Missouri and one lives outside the state, a question of where to file often comes up. In order to file in Missouri, the petitioner must have lived in Missouri for the most recent 90 days. Other states will also have minimum residency requirements, some longer than 90 days and some shorter. If both spouses meet the requirements for their respective states and children aren't involved, it becomes a race to the courthouse to see who files first.

Kids change the story quite a bit. In that case, working together under the Uniform Child Custody Jurisdiction Act, the courts in both states will determine which state makes the most sense. Key to this decision is where the children currently live and previously lived and for how long they resided in each place. The bottom line is that the divorce will get done in the state where most of the evidence regarding the welfare and support of the kids can be found (usually where they lived for the last six months).

And keep the children put once the divorce petition is filed. Without court approval, neither parent can move the youngsters from the Circuit Court's jurisdiction (out of the circuit). They must also remain at the address of the parent they primarily resided with during the 60 days before the filing date unless the mom and dad agree otherwise. If there is really a need to relocate, you had better work it out with the other parent.

Finally, each Circuit Court sets its own fee for filing a petition. The amount includes both state and local county charges. In some circuits the cost of delivering the petition to the other spouse is included, while in others it's collected separately.

Delivering the Dear John/Jane

So just how does a petition get to the other spouse? Well, to begin with, the petitioner gives the court an address where the other spouse lives or works or anywhere else the recipient is likely to be found.

Standard procedure is for a sheriff to hand deliver the petition to the respondent (this occurs about 10 days after the petition is filed). However, many lawyers use a private process server to do the job, and that's not a bad idea.

Some people react badly when confronted by a lawman (even though they are usually in plainclothes) shoving a document in their hand. Besides, unlike the sheriff, the process server will show up at the address at the specific time the petitioner says the other spouse is most likely to be there. Sheriffs go on their own schedules.

The petition doesn't have to be delivered directly to the other spouse. Any member of the respondent's family over 15 years old living at the given address will do. The sheriff or process server simply reports back to the court that the petition was served, and that is that. No signature by the respondent or whoever else might have received the document is required.

Delivery is really easy if both spouses retained lawyers prior to filing the petition. In this case the petitioner's lawyer simply contacts the other spouse's lawyer, who then agrees to a "waiver of necessity of service." That means no official service is necessary. The lawyer just mails it to the other lawyer, who then files a document with the court, and it's done.

Occasionally the petition is delivered by registered mail return receipt requested. The recipient then signs a form before a notary stating that the summons was received. This document is returned to a lawyer or directly to the court (if *pro se*). Don't worry, no rights are given up and no admission is being made if you are required to do this.

There's one last option. If the whereabouts of the spouse to be served are unknown, then the simplest method of notification is to publish the complaint in the classified section of the local newspaper for three weeks. Using fine print, this will only take up a few inches of a single column. The court will usually accept this publication as having served the petition as long as you can demonstrate that you first tried to locate the missing person. Remember to get proof that the notice ran for the required time period.

And the Answer, Please

Every petition requires a formal response, called an "answer," by the receiving spouse. Answers must be returned to the court within 30 days of the date the petition was served. In the answer the respondent either admits or denies what is stated in the petition. Frequently, the respondent's lawyer will deny in the answer certain facts that are stated in the petition just to force the other side to prove them. It's just common legal positioning leading, hopefully, to the negotiation of a final settlement.

Sometimes the respondent doesn't provide any answer. He or she just ignores everything. Despite the required 30-day response time, it's not against the law to ignore the petition. It simply sets in motion the default divorce process.

The default divorce procedure is more or less the same as the one used when both sides participate. The main difference is that only the petitioner is involved.

The good side of this situation is that, lacking any alternative argument, the petitioner will get a lot of what he or she asks for in the petition's request—namely, the child-related issues (legal and physical custody and child support) and the desired assets. However, equitable property division still applies. So, while you'll have no contradicting testimony, don't expect to get all the assets.

The downside to a default divorce is that it can lack finality. Later on, after the default judgment is in place, the do-nothing spouse may suddenly decide to do something. If the now-awakened former partner asks the court to set aside the earlier default settlement, the judge will often do just that. And then it's back to court so everyone can fight it out for real this time. Just one more thing that's not fair in this world.

But there's a limit to the court's tolerance. A defaulting spouse must challenge a default judgment within 12 months of the date it was issued. After a year, Missouri law prevents the default judgment from being set aside except under very unusual circumstances.

You're in the Army Now

Let's take a moment to thank our servicemen and women who are deployed around the world keeping this country safe. That's exactly what the federal government did in 2003 when it revamped the Servicemembers Civil Relief Act (the SCRA).

A major change provided by the updated SCRA is that it permits active-duty servicemembers unable to appear in a court or administrative proceeding due to their military duties to postpone the proceeding for a mandatory *minimum* of 90 days upon the servicemember's request. The petitioner must inform the court that the respondent is in active military service.

So if the spouse of an active servicemember in the Middle East or Europe or Asia wants a divorce, he or she may have to wait until the patriotic spouse returns from overseas (assuming the servicemember wants the delay). In this case everything is put on hold, and there can't be a default divorce.

Making Nice Nice

It really does take two to tango. No matter how you feel about your spouse, he or she is the one with whom you'll be hopefully negotiating a settlement. Maintaining a reasonably positive relationship can pay big dividends.

When kids are involved, it's likely you'll be dealing with each other for many years to come. Going out of your way to spoil things now will ensure even larger problems in the future.

So when filing the petition, it's wise to save the big surprises for another occasion. Let your spouse know what you're up to. Don't have the sheriff show up unexpectedly. And avoid serving the petition on your wedding anniversary or Valentine's Day. Using your mother-in-law's address for delivery is a judgment call but also not recommended.

And if you're the one receiving the petition (the respondent), understand that nothing is gained by behaving badly. The bottom line is that, with few exceptions, one spouse alone cannot stop the divorce from happening. Any attempt to sabotage or stall the event will only result in higher legal fees and hard feelings.

It's far better for both sides to simply concentrate on getting the best deal possible on the way out.

Money Makes the World Go 'Round

Divorce settlements are mostly about children and money. And a major portion of the child-related issues center on money. So it's important for the court (and your lawyer) to understand the financial condition of the marriage right from the start.

Most Circuit Courts require the petitioner's financial statement to be filed with the petition. The respondent will also have to provide similar financial documents either at the time of answering the petition or not too long thereafter. In any case, financial statements from both sides will definitely be needed if motions are entered for temporary orders (discussed in the *pendente lite* section below).

Your lawyer will give you the forms to fill out. They are also available on the website of the Office of State Courts Administrator (www.courts.mo.gov), or go to any of the commercial Internet websites (type "divorce in Missouri" in the search engine).

Each spouse will fill out a separate form. The required financial information includes the following:

1. The income of the party filling out the form. This should be based upon recent pay stubs, but also his or her income over the last three to five years depending on how volatile it has been (see the chapter on determining income).

2. The living expenses of the spouse filling out the form, including relevant child-care expenses.

3. A list of all the assets owned by the parties (not just

those owned by the party filling out the form). Indicate the estimated value of each asset and whose name is on the title or deed if there is one. Also indicate what assets were brought into the marriage and by which spouse. Smaller items can be grouped under such headings as household goods, etc. (see the chapters dealing with property).

4. List all debts, showing who loaned the money, the purpose of the loan (mortgage, car loan, etc.), the date it originated, the current outstanding balance, the monthly payments, and the name of the borrower.

Doing the Parenting Plan

If dependent children are part of the divorce, they are always the court's priority. Therefore, it's important to resolve the kid issues right away, at least on a temporary basis.

Parents are required to submit a "parenting plan" within 30 days of the service of process (which means 30 days after the day the respondent received the petition) or the filing of the entry of appearance (which means 30 days after the respondent's attorney filed a paper with the court acknowledging receipt of the petition). In general, the idea is to define each spouse's responsibilities (some or all can be joint responsibilities) with respect to the following matters:

1. The schedule showing when each parent will have the children in his or her care (this is called "physical custody").

2. Decision-making rights and responsibilities (this is called "legal custody" and refers to which parent decides on healthcare, schooling, after-school activities, etc.).

3. Dispute resolution (how disagreements between the parents regarding the kids will be settled if the parents can't solve them on their own).

4. Expenses of the children (the amount each parent must pay to support the children).

The parenting plan utilizes detailed forms that will be provided by your lawyer. They are also available on the website of the Office of State Courts Administrator (www.courts.mo.gov) or directly from the court. Just remember that these are only general forms. They may have to be adjusted to reflect the specifics of your family's needs.

From the same sources you'll also need to get a copy of Missouri's Presumed Child Support Guidelines and related worksheet along with a blank Form 14. Using this material, the amount of child support presumed by the state is calculated. Form 14 is then completed and supplied to the court along with the parenting plan.

Ideally, a single parenting plan is jointly developed by the parents. That's what the court likes to see. The plan's child-support proposal can be higher or lower than the calculation reported on Form 14. The judge is likely to approve any amount that is agreed to by both parties. However, if the parties disagree on the amount of child support or the parenting plan fails to address child support, the judge normally utilizes the support payments calculated using Form 14 (see child support chapter).

Couples who can't agree on a single parenting plan will have the judge decide for them on those issues as well. They should be prepared to live with a result that can easily be worse than anything they might have negotiated between themselves.

Only children who are the joint responsibility of both parents by either birth or adoption are included in the parenting plan. Children of one spouse for whom the other spouse has no legal obligation are not covered. Also, there's no requirement to provide a parenting plan for dependent children over the age of 18, but you can if you like.

Finally, the parenting plan doesn't have to represent the permanent structure regarding the kids. It's just until the final judgment is issued. Of course, if both sides want to make it the long-term plan, that's even better. Make sure the judge knows your intentions.

Okay, it's time to learn about the temporary orders.

Pendente Lite; No Carbs, No Calories

The divorce process takes time, especially if the parties don't see eye to eye on a lot of issues. During this period the court wants to be certain that no one, especially a child, suffers. So until there's a final judgment, an operating structure needs to be put in place.

The best way to develop one is for the spouses to negotiate a temporary plan without going to the courthouse. Smart couples who do this can usually avoid the entire temporary order process and the related expenses.

However, if they can't reach agreement on some or all of the issues, a judge will have to fill in the blanks. When issued by the court, this interim plan is called the PDL (an abbreviation for the Latin *pendente lite,* meaning "while the law case is pending") or more understandably, "temporary orders."

PDLs take into account the financial reports and the parenting plan(s) submitted earlier by the parties, as well as common requirements of the court. PDLs normally remain in place until the final divorce judgment is issued and usually specify some or all of the following:

1. All the important child-related issues, including child support (see the parenting plan section earlier).

2. Whether or not one of the parties will receive maintenance (alimony) and, if so, how much.

3. Who pays various debts (mortgage, car payments, credit cards, etc.) and operating expenses (electricity, heat, etc.).

4. Who stays in the marital home.

5. Protection of the assets from dissipation while the divorce is being decided (no unnecessary major purchases, loans, sale of property, etc.).

As much as possible, PDLs freeze the current situation until the final judgment sorts things out permanently. Under these temporary orders the spouses can be prevented from doing the following:

1. Canceling any health insurance (not allowed even if no temporary orders are issued).

2. Leaving Missouri permanently with the children. (With or without temporary orders, the children must remain at the address and with the parent they resided with for the 60 days prior to the filing of the divorce petition.)

3. Selling or disposing of any assets (except in the normal course of business).

4. Taking on any unusual debt. (You can still buy the groceries at Schnuck's with a credit card, but stay away from using it to charge a two-carat diamond ring or that hand-engraved Smith and Wesson.)

Sometimes these restrictions create an unintended hardship. One party might be in the process of selling a business, and the temporary orders (the PDL) are preventing the acceptance of a generous offer. Or perhaps funds have to be borrowed to stay out of bankruptcy. If the need is valid and timing is critical, it's possible to get relief from the court.

There's no time limit on when a PDL request must be made. So the spouses can first try to work things out on their own. If down the road they can't reach agreement, it's not too late to seek temporary orders from the court.

Remember, all the above arrangements (whether negotiated by the parties or decided by the judge) are temporary unless both sides want them to be permanent. Volunteering to be generous at this stage will often help you score some points with the judge.

In general, the court understands the difference between short term and long term. A stay-at-home mom may need a lot of bill-paying money from the dad "right now." Later on the judge may figure the mom should get a job and reduce the dad's payments.

Or the judge, seeing that the dad was able to make large payments under the temporary plan, may make them permanent when the divorce is finalized. So the best advice is to temper generosity with caution.

In summary, the easiest approach to resolving PDL issues is for the parties to work things out between themselves, using mediation, etc., if needed. Should that fail

and if they still want to avoid a hearing, the spouses (if
pro se) or their lawyers can meet with the judge in private
and try to resolve the undecided issues.

Hopefully that does the trick and their agreement is
implemented without a PDL being issued.

Yes, if the couple is determined to fight it out in court,
they can. But when they can't reach agreement on issues
that will last only a few months, how can they hope to
negotiate a permanent settlement? It's definitely a bad
omen.

Parents Need School, Too

In an effort to make both sides see the value of cooperation, the court insists that parents with dependent children attend a "parental educational class." The primary
objective of this training is to reduce the trauma of
divorce on the children

Each circuit has its own requirements for this class. In
some areas there's a charge; in others attendance is cour-
tesy of the local court. Parents don't have to attend
together and, in some circuits, are required to attend separately (you don't want warfare in the parent education
classroom).

The petitioner must attend the class within 45 days of
having submitted the petition. The respondent must
attend no later than 45 days after the petition was
received (or the filing of a voluntary waiver of service).

Make sure to send a certificate of attendance to your
lawyer or the court unless the class does it automatically. Don't start off on the wrong foot with the judge by
failing to show up.

Many circuits also have the power to require that couples with children try mediation to resolve the child-related issues. General exceptions to this rule are if the custody and visitation are uncontested (already agreed to by the parties) or one of the spouses has been found by the court to have abused the other spouse.

What to Do Next

Once the temporary arrangements are in place the focus becomes determining the permanent structure that will end up in the final judgment. The amount of additional work to be done is really up to the parties.

If the spouses have already reached a settlement covering all the issues, this agreement can be submitted to the court either directly or at the settlement conference (discussed below). Within 30 days the divorce should be granted.

Not all couples will be so lucky. At this point many spouses will still have unsettled items and the best approach, as always, is to reach an understanding outside of the courtroom. How they go about doing this depends on both the issues being contested and the nature of the individuals. In the end, some kind of compromise is usually part of the deal, and mediation can often help.

If asset distribution is the question, it may first be necessary to get valuable items or properties appraised. There's no point in sitting down to discuss the distribution of assets if the parties don't agree on what things are worth. On the other hand, professional appraisals are costly. Make sure the appraisal expense is not more than the value you hope to gain.

Also, if a court battle appears to be inevitable, this is the time to get ready for the final hearing. Child-custody fights in particular take a lot of preparation. Statements need to be collected from doctors, teachers, therapists, neighbors, friends, relatives, etc., who support the points of view of the respective parties. Psychological evaluations of the parents or possibly the entire family may be performed as well.

Meanwhile, things can come up that require prompt and definitive action by the court. For example, one spouse is not allowing the visitation rights specified in the temporary orders, or visitation rights are being abused. The well-behaved spouse can file an enforcement ("family access") motion requesting that the judge get things back on track. The actions of the troublemaker may also get reflected in the final judgment. So don't get the judge angry.

Discovering Information

Frequently, one spouse will have information related to the divorce that the other spouse wants. In simple situations, it may be enough to rely on what you know or on what your spouse tells you. But often, it's important to collect critical information under oath.

Missouri law gives each party the right to know all the facts relevant to the divorce that the other party knows. The process of collecting this information is referred to as "discovery," and it's primarily available in three flavors.

Interrogatories—These are written questions to the opposing spouse. They must be responded to in writing and under oath within 30 days. Your lawyer will review any questions you receive to ensure they meet the legal requirements and help you prepare your answers in a proper form. Be aware that in some circuits, you'll be required to give your own answers, in advance, to any questions that you ask your spouse, as if the question had been asked of you.

Depositions—A spouse also has the right to directly question the other spouse and other witnesses (neighbors, teachers, lovers, etc.) under oath, usually at an attorney's office. Lawyers for both sides will be there to ask questions, and it will sound a lot like a courtroom except there isn't a judge. The questions and answers are taken down by a court reporter and can be submitted to the court as evidence. Depositions are also the way each of the spouses can get records from third parties, such as employers, schools, banks, etc.

Request for Production of Documents—This has to do with asking the other spouse to provide key documents. Often they are related to financial and property issues (canceled checks, bank statements, income tax returns, credit card information, stock information, business records, property titles, receipts, etc.). Non-financial documents can be requested as well.

Now, just because one side asks for information doesn't mean it has to be provided. There are limits to what each party is entitled to receive. It's possible to argue that something is not relevant or that the time or cost to produce the information (including expensive depositions) is greater than its value. In these cases an objection should be filed with the court to have the request denied.

For example, while a demand for three years of credit card statements is reasonable, it's unlikely the court would support the need for 15 years of statements.

In addition to the major three discovery categories, there are a few more including the following:

Request for Admission—One side asks the other side to admit certain facts. If the party receiving the request fails to respond on a timely basis, it's assumed by the court that the facts are admitted.

Request for Entry upon Land—One party's request to inspect the marital home or other property controlled by the other spouse. This could include inspection of a private business site run by that spouse to check the records or count the inventory.

One moment, please. If you've read this discovery discussion without feeling the dollar bills flying out of your pocket, you just weren't paying close attention. Try to settle things fairly with as little legal intrigue and jousting around as possible. Now back to the story.

The Settlement Conference

Sometime in the process, either during discovery or right after the discovery elements are completed, a settlement conference is often held in the judge's chambers or, in some instances, in the courtroom. The purpose is to see if the divorce can be settled without going to trial.

While spouses are usually required to attend, normally only their lawyers will speak with the judge. Of course, if the parties aren't using lawyers, it's up to them to talk things over with the judge. Please don't bring along the kids.

Remember, this isn't a trial, and the judge isn't there to decide the case. It's just a meeting to report on what progress has been made and if the two sides are likely to reach a settlement. At the settlement conference, one of three things is going to happen.

1. Both sides will report to the judge that everything has been decided, right down to who gets Aunt Martha's antique quilt, or that such complete agreement is expected to be reached shortly. In this case the judge will be happy and, after reviewing the main settlement issues, set a deadline to make final submissions to the court.

2. The parties can report that while a settlement is not at hand, the spouses want to continue to try to reach one. In this case the judge may (not always) provide some insight into his or her views on the key issues. This helps the sides understand how the court is likely to decide if they fail to reach an out-of-court agreement. A second settlement conference will be scheduled while the couple continues the negotiations. Sometimes up to four settlement conferences are required, but that's still better than going to trial.

3. The judge can decide to set a trial date to move the case along, especially if it looks like the case won't settle easily. This doesn't necessarily mean the spouses should stop talking. Sometimes setting a court date will motivate a difficult party to be more willing to compromise. Not infrequently, a judge will set another settlement conference as well as a trial date. That way, if things don't get worked out the next time around, everyone knows that a trial is looming.

Avoiding a Trial

Everyone in the Missouri court system wants divorcing couples to reach an out-of-court settlement. Over 90% do just that. Fail to join this lucky majority, and there's an expensive, exasperating, and definitely uncertain trial in the future.

Assuming the two parties are able to negotiate a complete settlement, the next steps are easy and relatively painless. All the terms get written up into a signed and witnessed document called a "settlement agreement" or "separation agreement." It's then submitted to the court for the judge's signature.

Most judges will issue a final judgment based on the submitted documents, but some, even if they see no particular problem with the affidavits, insist upon a hearing if children are involved.

If minor or dependent children are involved, the parenting plan and a completed Form 14 (the child-support calculation discussed earlier in this chapter) are also provided at this time unless they were delivered earlier. The court wants to make sure that the well-being of the children is reasonably protected. In particular, while the proposed amount of child support can be less than the Missouri guidelines, it must not appear to the judge to be unjust or inappropriate.

But don't expect the court to consider whether each spouse has received a fair deal on the rest of the issues. The judge will assume that the attorneys ensured that the agreement is equitable for their clients. Only if the judge suspects "foul play" would the court question an out of court settlement. That's a very unusual event.

The final steps vary depending on which circuit is involved. Usually, if an "affidavit for judgment" (a sworn statement of what the parties would have said if they'd had to appear in court) is submitted along with the separation agreement and parenting plan, there's no need for anyone to appear in court. In a matter of days, the judge will issue a final judgment reflecting the conditions contained in the separation agreement and the parenting plan. You're officially divorced when this judgment is signed by the judge.

Sometimes the judge wants the submitted documents altered. For example, the parenting plan may fail to cover important child issues. The parties usually comply by submitting a revised agreement. Only if there are major issues would a court appearance be required.

Here Comes the Judge!

But some couples are bound and determined to have their day in court, even if they regret it later on. So how long does it take to actually get in front of a judge? Well, unlike many states, Missouri wants things to move pretty quickly. In fact, the Missouri Supreme Court prefers divorces to be resolved within a year. Many are done much faster.

While each circuit has its own procedure, judges work hard to arrange a trial date as soon as possible. If the receiving spouse refuses to answer the petition, the court date can be set 30 days following the date the petition was served (default divorce).

Some circuits do things in two steps. An initial court date is set, at which time the actual date of the trial is then scheduled. With other circuits the initial court date is when the trial actually takes place. If you want to know the specific rules used by your circuit, check out the Missouri Bar's website, www.mobar.org. As mentioned earlier, it's also possible to set the trial date at the settlement conference (see the above discussion).

One thing the spouses should almost always do before getting the trial date is to be certain that they have gone as far as they can with their out-of-court negotiations. Give mediation, Collaborative Practice (both discussed later in this book), or other dispute resolution approaches a try. Remember, going to court is usually not your best hope. It is simply the penalty for failure.

Nevertheless, if the spouses have their caps set for court, they first need to figure out the amount of courtroom time required. If everything is agreed to between the parties except who gets the kids on Christmas, a judge can figure that out in a short time. But if all the issues are undecided, then a major time slot of around two or three days is likely to be required—maybe longer if several expert witnesses are involved.

Naturally, it's easier to find an hour in a court's schedule than three days so the little trials get scheduled and completed sooner. For longer time requirements, the court can break the trial into parts (referred to as "bifurcated proceedings"). Perhaps the child custody and support issues will be handled one day and everything else at another time. While not used very often, it remains an option.

The bottom line is that the more time your case requires, the longer you will usually wait before going to trial. Big divorces may take six months or more to get heard. This waiting period is from the time the trial is requested, not from the date of the petition, which may have been submitted months earlier.

Keep in mind the alternative stated earlier. If all the issues are agreed to out of court, there will be no trial. At most, both spouses will go before the judge for five to ten minutes and it's over.

And that's a good thing.

Legal Separation vs. Divorce

Now that the basic divorce process has been covered let's look at an important option.

Some petitioners may not be seeking a divorce at all. The unhappy spouse just wants the other partner out of his or her day-to-day life.

Often a religious restriction exists regarding divorce. Perhaps there's concern that medical or other benefits will be lost. The tax advantages of staying married can be important. A romantic might feel that by putting some distance and structure between the warring spouses, they might calm down enough to give it another try.

Under a legal separation almost all the elements of divorce exist. The couple is able to live separate and apart. Child custody and child support get worked out. Assets and debts are divided up, including who gets the family home. There's even the possibility of maintenance (alimony).

What's different is that the spouses remain spouses. They are still legally married.

The process is basically identical to getting a divorce. Instead of asking to end the marriage, the petition requests a legal separation. The legal separation petition reads almost exactly the same as a petition for dissolution, with one important difference: The petitioner has to claim that the marriage is *not* irretrievably broken. The petition must be answered in agreement by the other spouse. Settlement conferences and courtroom sessions work the same, as well.

Another path exists that can also lead to a legal separation. This occurs when one side wants a divorce (and filed a petition for one) while the other wants to remain hitched. It's possible for the spouse who's against the divorce to convince the court that the marriage hasn't irretrievably broken down. In such a case the judge may deny the petition seeking a divorce and grant a legal separation instead.

But this is a rare situation. And if 90 days later there hasn't been a reconciliation, the court is certain to approve the divorce. The state just can't force people to love each other or merely to like each other.

Finally, even if a husband and wife have agreed to a legal separation, either one of them can ask the judge to change the legal separation to a dissolution after 90 days have gone by.

OK, Do It Yourself

Still want to do a divorce on your own (called *pro se* and pronounced pro say)? If the issues are not complex (hopefully there are no issues), the process is not overly difficult.

Either you or your spouse kicks things off by filing a divorce petition with the Circuit Court (forms and instructions can be obtained by going to the Missouri Court website www.courts.mo.gov and clicking on "Representing Yourself"). This website provides a lot of additional *pro se* information as well. Assuming everyone is cooperating, the court should soon receive the answer to the petition from the other spouse.

At about the same time, both sides need to submit the parenting plan along with a completed Form 14 to the court. If the parties are in agreement on the temporary issues, they can usually operate informally for the time being. However, if they can't agree, the PDL orders (temporary orders) will be issued.

The next thing to do is to arrange for a settlement conference and hopefully finalize the details with the judge. If children are involved, don't forget about attending the parental educational class discussed earlier.

Once everything is settled, submit the agreement to the Circuit Court. A judge will review it and in as little as a couple of days, assuming it's 30 days after the petition filing date (the required waiting period for no-fault divorces), the divorce should be granted.

It's not necessary that *pro se* parties agree to everything right away. Arrangements for child support and maintenance can be stipulated by the spouses or determined by the court and issued in the temporary orders. Meanwhile, the couple goes off to negotiate the rest. If these differences can't be resolved privately, they can fight it out in court (just like they could if they had lawyers).

It's clear that when things are very simple and both sides agree on the settlement, a couple can get away with doing it on their own. However, under those circumstances the cost of using lawyers would be very reasonable anyway.

Wouldn't it be comforting to have a little professional advice to ensure that nothing important is being overlooked? It's not necessarily up to the judge to point out such missed opportunities.

Frankly, if the parties are in dispute over important matters, the assistance of lawyers is highly recommended.

"It Ain't Over Till It's Over"

OK, two Yogi Berra quotes in one chapter is enough! Anyway, even when the final judgment is issued, things may not be entirely over.

That's because the order isn't really final until 30 days after it's issued. During that period either party can go back to the judge and point out an "error" in the order. Such mistakes can relate to the division of assets and debt, child custody and support, and anything else.

For example, the judge may have used an incorrect value on an asset. Or the order may have failed to cover who gets the kids for their birthdays. It's also not unusual for

the parties to suddenly realize that they can come up
with better arrangements than the judge did. Now is the
time for them to get any last-minute changes they negotiate into the order.

Just make sure to submit such requests within 30 days of
the final judgment date. Remember, these are calendar
days, with an extra day or two should the thirtieth day
be a holiday or weekend. Hopefully, the judge will
agree to change or correct the order as requested.
However, this is definitely not a no news is good news
situation. If the judge fails to respond to the request in
90 days, you lose. The judgment becomes final as it was
originally issued.

Caution!! Believe it or not, the law isn't 100% clear on
whether the parties may get married during this 30-day
notification period. So it's best to hold off.

Maybe It's Still Not Over

It's also possible to appeal the final divorce order. An
appeal is not another trial. New evidence can't be introduced. The final judgment will be overturned only if the
original judge disregarded the law or demonstrated
"abuse of discretion" (meaning that the judge's ruling,
while not in violation of the law, was substantially
unreasonable).

Appeals are made to the Missouri Court of Appeals and
not the Circuit Court. There's a filing fee, and you'll be
required to pay for a transcript of the court proceedings
and a compilation of the original trial documents and
exhibits. Expect these to cost a few hundred to a few
thousand dollars. But that's just the beginning. You may
spend as much on your appeal as you did on your initial
divorce.

In the end the large majority of appeals fail. That's because the Court of Appeals really hates to overrule the Circuit Court. The original Circuit Court judge has a lot of discretion, and his or her ruling reflects not only the facts on paper, but also the gut feeling the judge has upon seeing both spouses in court.

That's something the judges in the appellate court rarely experience. Most of the appeal process is done strictly on paper, with only a short oral argument. So unless there's something really out of whack, the chances of success are not great.

An appeal must be filed within ten days of the original judgment becoming final. Miss that date and it's usually too late. Expect it to take six to twelve months to get the appeal reviewed. During that time the final judgment will still be enforced unless the appealing spouse posts a "bond" (a sum of money in an amount set by the judge). Regardless, custody and child-support orders will almost always be enforced during the appeal process.

A successful appeal generally relies on the appealing party having a very solid understanding of the law. People can and do appeal final orders without using a lawyer, but that's a very difficult row to hoe.

Is It Ever Really Over

In most cases, divorce will not end the relationship with your spouse. It merely changes it. Depending on the complexity of the marriage in terms of length, money, assets, and children, it's possible that the two of you will be interacting for many, many years after the divorce becomes final.

The final divorce judgment itself is subject to modification as situations change over time. However, some items are more difficult to adjust than others.

The most difficult to alter is the division of assets (think of it as being etched in stone). Unless one side can show that the other party lied or intentionally withheld critical information about the existence or worth of certain valuables, it's extremely hard to alter the property distribution once it's final.

This is why it's so important to know your rights to all the assets before agreeing to a split. The court will not change things later on just because you made a bad deal!

Maintenance (alimony) may be more open to adjustment in the future, but only if the original maintenance order is called "modifiable" in the final judgment (meaning it can be changed by the court in the future). If it is and circumstances develop that make the original payments either inadequate or unreasonably high, a party can ask the court to adjust the payments. It's also possible to have the maintenance payments terminated. Either of these requests is called a "motion to modify." While not an easy process, the final order is not necessarily cast in cement when it comes to spousal support.

The same is true for child custody rights. Things change. The loving father who was getting the children 30% of the time has become a drug addict or a child abuser. The infant who was spending most of his time with his mother now is ready to have more overnights with his father. If such allegations are proven in court, alterations to the custody order can be made (custody rights are always modifiable).

By far the most flexible item is child support. The court will be very willing to recognize a change in circumstances that makes the current arrangement unfair or inadequate. By now you should realize that the number one priority in a Missouri divorce is the children. So don't be surprised if from time to time adjustments are required.

That being said, the decision will rely largely upon the child support guideline calculation (see the child support chapter). Sometimes parents are surprised at how much change is required to justify a 20% increase or decrease which is generally the minimum child support alteration the court will consider.

Divorce Is What You Make It

How complicated and miserable the divorce process becomes is entirely up to the two parties. It takes the effort of both sides to make it a reasonably bearable experience. It requires only one difficult spouse to bring everything down into the dirt.

But don't think for one minute that you can take your partner down while keeping your own knees clean. Frankly, that is one of the ways lawyers earn their keep. They are there to protect their clients.

If one side is going to act unreasonably, then the opposing lawyer's job is to make certain that it's an unsuccessful effort (and get the court to have the troublemaking spouse pay all the extra legal fees).

Time and again this book stresses compromise. Things will most likely all end up at some reasonable conclusion no matter how long the journey. So why should either party see a benefit in trying to make the road a miserable one? Take the high road!

NOTE: See the summary of Missouri's divorce process, along with a flow chart diagram in the Appendix.

CHAPTER 3

Finding and Using a Lawyer

"Lawyer" Isn't a Four-Letter Word

T HERE'S NO QUESTION about it; you don't need a lawyer in order to get a divorce. Missouri law clearly provides for *pro se* representation (meaning representing yourself and pronounced "pro say"). However, the law isn't simpler and less sophisticated just because you're doing it alone. Not having an attorney means exactly what it sounds like. You'd better understand how to start, where to go, and what to do.

Do you know the definition of marital assets and the rules governing their distribution? Is Public School Retirement dealt with differently from a pension or 401(k) account? What about assets acquired before the marriage or during the separation? How can you ensure getting fair custody rights with your children? How much maintenance (alimony) should you receive or pay? What if you are disabled?

The list of complex issues is a long one. Reading this book will help, but success depends mostly on your per-

46

sonal experience. What experience, you ask? Well, that's the point. Think about getting a lawyer.

Keep in mind that there's a lot at risk. The fallout from a divorce decree lasts a lifetime. It determines the quality of life that you and your children will enjoy (or not enjoy). It can mean the difference between living happily ever after or living with regret.

When the divorcing couple is wealthy, the need for a lawyer seems more obvious. In fact, parties in a marriage operating on a tight budget usually have an even greater need for legal counsel.

The mother in Moberly raising three kids and working in a local grocery store can't afford to miss out on an extra few hundred dollars of monthly maintenance. The father needs to be sure that something is left for him after those support payments are made and the assets split up (not to mention the child custody rights, etc.).

Now compare that to the rich man's world. If one side overpays or underreceives a few hundred thousand dollars in a multimillion-dollar divorce settlement, life will still go on in a pretty nice way. So who needs a lawyer more, those with big incomes or those with modest ones?

Finding a Raindrop in the Sea

There are about 25,000 lawyers practicing in Missouri today. That's just over one lawyer for every 225 residents. However, not every attorney will be the right one for you.

Practice makes perfect, whether it's a dentist doing root canals or a lawyer representing divorcing clients. So the first thing to look for is an attorney with a good portion of his or her practice focused on family law. The number of divorce cases a lawyer handles each year gives some indication of that focus.

However, don't rely only on the total number of divorces. An attorney who is involved in three or four big divorces a year may be more knowledgeable than a lawyer doing 20 simple ones. Use a little judgment. Good lawyers will clearly lay out their qualifications and let you know whether or not divorce is their "thing."

And in most cases their thing should be negotiation and not going into court with six-guns ablaze. TV shows from *Perry Mason* to *Law and Order* glamorize litigation lawyers, but is that really what you need? It's better to find an attorney who thinks first of settlement (negotiation) but can fight it out in front of a judge if required. Don't forget, over 90% of divorces are going to settle out of court.

You may already have a relationship with a lawyer. Perhaps one did some work for you regarding your business, the closing on your house, a will, or a family member's DUI arrest.

The fact that an attorney was great at handling the refinancing of your auto body business doesn't necessarily qualify him or her to take on your divorce. Also, using a family lawyer who has a long-term relationship with both marriage partners may create at least an awkward situation and perhaps a conflict of interest.

Recommendations are a great way to enhance your search. They can come from friends and friends of friends. They can also come from other lawyers (including your family lawyer) who either don't do divorces or are too busy to take on your case. Just remember to look beyond the recommendation. Does the person making the recommendation understand your needs? If he or she used the same lawyer for a divorce, was it a situation similar to your own?

The final test will be when you actually sit down in the lawyer's office for your first meeting. Does the lawyer ask you what your goals are or tell you what they should be? Are process options (mediation, Collaborative Divorce, etc.) discussed?

Is the attorney someone you can be open and honest with over the long term? This lawyer will be spending your money. Are you comfortable with that? There should be no doubt about matters of ethics or judgment. Do you get the feeling that he or she is a professional and a winner?

If the answers to these questions are all positive, you've found your legal representative. But should the meeting not go well, don't hesitate to say "Thanks, but no thanks." It's far better to nip things in the bud than to go on for many months (and many dollars) before finally facing the fact that you're not a happy camper.

A Local Yokel

Some people wonder whether it's better to hire a local lawyer with local knowledge (a Butler lawyer for a Butler divorce, for example) versus hiring a "big gun" from Kansas City (all lawyers from Kansas City and St. Louis, too, think they're big guns). Well, the first thing to remember is that there are good lawyers everywhere in Missouri. Many simply prefer more rural surroundings rather than life in the city.

A local lawyer will usually have a closer relationship with the local Circuit Court clerks and this does give them a slight advantage. A good rapport with these process facilitators can go a long way in making things move smoothly.

On a practical basis, the main reason for using a local attorney is cost. Lawyers usually charge for travel time at the same rate they charge for standing before a judge. If your Kansas City attorney has to drive 65 miles down highway 71 to Butler, you'll be paying for that time plus expenses.

By the way, Butler has some pretty good lawyers.

Structuring the Game Plan

The next step is to settle on a plan for using your lawyer. Of course, there's the traditional way where the attorney does just about everything. This can work fine, but it has some drawbacks. The first is that it's the most expensive approach (see the discussion on costs below). Second, it can prolong the divorce process and may not result in the best final settlement.

Remember, at the start, your lawyer usually doesn't know you or your spouse very well. While an experienced attorney can get up the learning curve pretty quickly, he or she may never understand all the fine points of your marital relationship. How could anyone, except the parties to the marriage, know the hidden meanings in each other's body language and keywords? Who knows your spouse better than you do?

So it's usually better not to give up talking and negotiating with your spouse just because you have a lawyer. It's likely that the marriage partners can come up with more acceptable solutions to most issues than will their attorneys.

Of course, this assumes that both sides really want to find a fair solution. Frankly, if they don't (or one of the two doesn't), then it's unlikely that the lawyers will have much success finding one.

This inevitably leads to the worst-case situation where everything is left up to the judge, who doesn't know either of you from Adam. He or she will decide how you live the rest of your life. Maybe you'll get what you want and maybe not.

Remember, if you enter the divorce process thinking you're going to gain and the other side is going to lose, it will likely be a very long, painful, and disappointing event. A good lawyer simply will not allow such a lop-sided victory to occur. So think of winning in terms of ending in a tie score. No one is delighted, but everyone survives.

A big exception to this discussion is if one party is being abused by the other. In this situation, the abused spouse is not in a position to represent him- or herself in any discussions. The lawyers can work things out (even if it means going to court) while the abused spouse looks forward to a life free from further torment.

It's Not Funny Money, Honey

In Missouri you can generally expect to pay a lawyer between $150 and $350 an hour for working on your divorce (some are much higher and a few lower). Rates vary, based on the location in the state, the experience of the lawyer, and how busy he or she is. Most attorneys will be in the middle part of the range ($175 to $300).

Typically, legal services are paid for in advance, but this doesn't mean the total cost is paid up front. Depending on the complexity of the divorce, the amount collected after the first meeting will range from a few hundred to a few thousand dollars (called a retainer). As the retainer gets used up, additional amounts will be requested in order to top up your account. Hopefully, a positive balance is maintained throughout the process.

Sometimes one spouse has access to significantly more money than the other. The "poor" spouse can ask the court, often in the temporary-orders motion (the PDL), to require the other party to pay some or all of the poorer one's legal fees. Be sure to discuss this possibility with your attorney.

Despite the jokes and "shark stories," most lawyers do have hearts. Many lawyers will make arrangement to spread the costs over an extended time or wait to collect until you receive money from your spouse. Keep in mind, though, that you have a lot of control over how expensive your divorce gets. Try limiting the number of calls you make and e-mails you send to your lawyer and keep your requests reasonable

Dialing for Dollars

How easy is it to run up expenses? Well, consider the cost of a simple ten-minute phone call. As mentioned before, many clients stop communicating directly with their spouses once a lawyer is obtained. They prefer to have their attorney do the talking for them. But your lawyer will not communicate directly with your spouse either. Instead, he or she will contact your spouse's attorney, who in turn relays the discussion to your spouse.

The costs generated by this approach are obvious. Lawyers generally have minimum charges for making calls and sending letters. It is common for telephone calls to be charged in six-minute increments. So if a lawyer makes a ten-minute phone call on your behalf, you will usually be charged a minimum of 12 minutes (two-tenths of an hour).

Since your lawyer is talking to your spouse's attorney (who will be charging your spouse for the same 12 minutes), you need to double the cost of the phone call.

Following that call, both attorneys will probably need to notify their clients of what was discussed. So add on the cost of two more phone calls. After the lawyers check with you and your spouse, an additional phone call may be required between the two attorneys to finalize things.

And don't forget that an attorney may spend a few minutes writing up notes after each conversation. That's more money out of your pocket.

In the end, the cost to you and your spouse for these brief discussions could easily total an hour of legal fees. That might be as much as $250 to $300 or more! It would have cost nothing if you had talked about the issue directly with your spouse, and it's far more likely that a resolution would have been reached.

However in some situations, it's better to have the lawyers work things out. This is particularly true if the discussion involves points of law, structuring the agreement, or the actual legal process of the divorce. Yet so many things can be discussed directly between the parties. As you see, the price for failing to do so can be quite breathtaking.

By now you're probably thinking that while it's a good idea to have an attorney, there is no way you can afford one. The miracle is that you probably *can* afford one. If both sides are cooperative and no issues are contested (please note the words "no issues"), it's possible for the total cost per lawyer to be as low as $750 in smaller towns and up to between $1,500 and $2,500 in the larger cities.

Remember that the lawyers have done this before and are well organized to efficiently manage the process. Their assistants (who are charged out at a lower rate) know the routine and can do much of the work. The lawyers will address those areas that require their special training and expertise.

And the Final Bill, Please

If divorces were not so painfully personal most of them could be completed with little effort. The old expressions, "You can't get blood from a turnip" and "There's no free lunch" apply in spades when it comes to divorce. So in the end, settlements are generally fair to both sides. Unfortunately, bitterness, pettiness, and pure illogical behavior can make the road leading to this reasonable conclusion a long and costly one.

Just how much a contested divorce costs is hard to say because there are so many variables. You can be certain that expenses rise rapidly anytime the parties disagree on an issue. For example, if they fail to settle on the value of a house and hire separate appraisers, the combined appraisal fees may be $700 to $1000. If it's a commercial building, each appraisal might cost $2,000 or more. Child custody fights can take on an economic life of their own (see the child custody chapter). Every additional issue becomes surrounded by dollar signs.

Even if there are only a few items in dispute, you can expect an additional $1,000 to $5,000 for legal and service fees. If things really get out of hand, it can cost in excess of $100,000 for each side to cover the costs of lawyers and the other professionals involved in such matters. The sad part is that it takes only one unreasonable party to make these skyrocketing expenses unavoidable. Of course, if the couple lacks such lofty funds, the incentive to compromise is great.

One last thought on how to keep costs down. If you can't work out a deal with your spouse on your own, try mediation. Mediation can be a lot less expensive than doing the "full monty" (turning over everything to the two lawyers) and far less costly than going to court. The lawyers still have a role to play, but it will require less of their expensive time (see the chapter on mediation).

There's also a chapter on Collaborative Practice. This is a more complex and expensive process than mediation, but it's definitely more economical than going to trial.

Besides the money saved, mediation and Collaborative Practice procedures usually result in settlements that are much more satisfying to both sides than what the court might order. In the end, the parties have to decide whose kids' college education they want to pay for—their own or their lawyers'.

The First Meeting with Your Lawyer

The first part of this chapter provided an overview on acquiring and using an attorney. Now let's get into the details as they relate to the initial meeting.

Making the first appointment to see a lawyer doesn't imply a final commitment. However, based on recommendations and reputation, you should already be pretty confident that he or she is a good choice.

Talking directly to the attorney when you call to set the meeting date will allow for a quick one-on-one evaluation. Ask about first-meeting charges and the hourly rate so that there are no surprises. If you have a good reason for needing a break on the fees, don't hesitate to mention it at the time of your telephone call. You might as well know right away whether or not the attorney is willing to consider an adjustment.

First meeting costs can vary. A lawyer may not charge for a 15- or 20-minute chat just to see if you want to go ahead. However, to get into the detail may take between one and two hours depending on the complexity of the divorce. In this case most attorneys require some payment in order to make sure that the potential client is not just "window shopping." The amount can be a fixed fee or simply the hourly rate for however long the meeting lasts.

Being prepared and organized can greatly reduce the time required and increase the productivity of the meeting. Strive to accomplish the following objectives:

1. *Evaluate the Lawyer*—Determine whether you're satisfied with the lawyer's experience in handling divorces similar to your own situation. Are you compatible? How well will you be able to work together?

2. *Discuss the Issues*—You will need to give the lawyer a complete overview of the issues surrounding the divorce (see the meeting efficiency section below). Make note of the questions you can't answer on the spot and submit responses by telephone, e-mail, or letter.

3. *Understand the Process*—The lawyer should outline the divorce process and review the legal rights of the parties. This will give you a sense of direction, timing, and a general idea of the likely settlement terms.

4. *Develop the Game Plan*—Establish your objectives and work out a game plan to reach them. This includes deciding who will do what. Make sure you feel comfortable with how matters will proceed. While the attorney is an expert on the law, you know the situation best. This is the time to voice your opinions and concerns. Agree on what actions you will be notified about before they are taken by the lawyer (limits on spending, agreeing to meetings, telephone calls, etc.).

5. *Understand the Costs*—The lawyer should clearly lay out all the potential costs related to the divorce and the

billing policy of the firm, including the required retainer. Discuss the hourly rates charged for the lawyer and paralegal, the cost for copying documents, the minimum billing amounts for telephone calls and preparing letters, etc. Remember to address special payment requests you feel are necessary (credit terms, etc.).

6. *Agree on Proceeding*—By the end of the meeting the lawyer will either decide to take the case or suggest another option. Unless unexpected issues or a conflict of interest are revealed, it's most likely that the attorney will take the case. However, if for some reason you're not satisfied, there is nothing wrong in saying so. Remember, divorce is a growth industry. If the lawyer is good, there will be other clients who make a better match.

Shortly after the meeting (assuming you agree to go forward), the lawyer should provide you with a document outlining all the issues agreed to at the first meeting, including a fee schedule, credit policy, the retainer, etc. It will also clearly state what you are paying the lawyer to do. In this case it will be to handle only your divorce. It may also say what the lawyer is not doing (for example, "the lawyer is not providing any tax advice").

Meeting Efficiency, or Getting the Most for Your Money

At your first meeting the lawyer will be like a computer searching for data. The attorney already has the operating software (the law, the legal process, how to present a case, etc.). Your job is to enter into this system all the facts related to your situation.

But just like a computer, if you provide incorrect, incomplete or misleading data, then you can't expect the results to be satisfactory. Eventually, it will get sorted out, but you'll have added substantial expense to the processes. In addition, opportunities to get a better settlement may be lost.

So come to the initial meeting fully prepared. This isn't the time to get carried away with bitterness or sarcasm about your spouse. Your attorney is looking for factual information and constructive ideas. All the emotional stuff just takes up valuable time. If you must cry on someone's shoulder, try to do it with a friend who isn't charging you $275 an hour. Hey, it's your money.

At the initial meeting bring along the following written information:

1. The names, dates of birth, Social Security numbers, addresses/telephone numbers for you, your spouse, and the children. You might include a short biography of each member of the family in order to make the individuals come to life for the lawyer.

2. Copies of all relevant legal documents, such as prenuptial agreements, restraining orders, etc.

3. Any proposal or correspondence that you exchanged with your spouse regarding settlement issues.

4. Tax returns for the last three years and pay stubs for the last three months.

5. A list of all the major assets that you and your spouse possess. Indicate whose name each item is owned under and its estimated resale value (this value may be more or less than what you paid). Household furnishings can be lumped together under a single estimated value. And don't forget to put down how much money you owe on each item (indicate the monthly payments and how long before each will be paid off). List any other debt you and your spouse have, such as credit card balances, etc.

Finally, give a general list of any significant funds or assets that either spouse brought into the marriage.

6. A time line of events covering all important activities leading up to the decision to divorce. This is one of the best ways of getting your story across to the attorney. It's simply a list of key events in date order that are relevant to the divorce. Remember at this first meeting you are giving the lawyer a ton of data about a family he or she has never heard of before. The time line helps eliminate confusion.

7. If you're the one filing the petition, don't forget to bring the information required to fill out a petition, listed in the chapter on Missouri's divorce process.

The lawyer will take a lot of notes at the meeting and so should you. Get a binder or some other kind of filing system, and keep all notes and documents in one place. If being organized is not your strength in day-to-day living, try to make this an exception. After all, the divorce settlement is likely to have a tremendous impact on your relationship with your children, as well as possibly being the most important financial event of your life.

Changing Your Lawyer

Even when things look good at the start, along the way you may become unhappy with the lawyer you selected. While there's no obligation to continue this relationship, making such a midstream change should be done only after careful consideration. Remember, new representation will not improve the facts in your case.

But if you're not able to resolve the problem with your attorney, don't feel uncomfortable about making the change. It's also okay to seek a second opinion. You may discover that your lawyer is doing a good job, or you may find out that your concerns about your lawyer are justified. And don't worry about offending your attorney by talking to someone else. For what you're paying you deserve to feel confident that you've made the right decision.

On the other hand, a party who is into his or her third or fourth lawyer risks giving a poor impression to the judge.

What about Sharing a Lawyer

One lawyer cannot represent two opposing clients. So if just one lawyer is used, that attorney is representing only one of the parties, and the other party has no representation. This works best when both sides have already reached a clear understanding on the settlement issues. Hopefully, there are no issues or in the worst case they are very simple ones.

For example, a couple in Kirksville was married for a short time when they decided to separate. Never bothering to get divorced, they lived apart for almost ten years. Then one day the husband decided to marry his girlfriend (more her decision than his), but first he needed a divorce.

He and his wife had been living successful and quite separate lives for a long time. Virtually all their assets were acquired after the separation. Best of all, there was no hostility between them. In fact, they enjoyed each other's company.

The husband hired a lawyer who drew up a settlement agreement based on the desires of both parties. The wife signed the required documents prepared by his lawyer, who then filed them with the court. The divorce was granted only a few days later. The ex-wife was invited to the couple's wedding.

In this case, the lawyer made it clear to the wife that he was representing only the husband. Such an approach required a good deal of trust on the part of the wife, since she had little protection under the law if she made a bad deal. It would be unethical for the husband's attorney to advise her on what to do.

The judge was also under no obligation to point out an opportunity the wife may be giving up by agreeing to the proposed settlement. In this particular divorce the results were quite satisfactory and the legal bills very low.

Keep in mind that this story is about one side having a lawyer and one side having no lawyer. They are not sharing a lawyer. Divorcing parties can't share an attorney.

So, Is a Lawyer Really Necessary

Read this book and then decide if you need a lawyer. Remember, it's often a matter of "pay me now or pay me later." And it's far cheaper for someone to have an attorney work out a fair settlement before the divorce than to have him or her try to fix a bad final judgment.

Nevertheless, if you decide to handle your own divorce (a "*pro se*" divorce), some key points in this chapter are still very useful. After all, you'll need to be as prepared as any lawyer would be if you expect to succeed.

1. Get all the details of your marriage organized properly (time line, asset valuation, debt details, legal and tax documents, etc.).

2. Keep detailed notes of all relevant conversations and proposals.

3. Try to settle things with your spouse out of court.

Finally, some people who wish to do a *pro se* divorce will still employ a lawyer as a consultant for particular issues. Under this arrangement the attorney is used only to provide information on certain areas of the law and to review documents before signing, etc. Most of the work is done by the spouses.

Depending on the complexity of the divorce and how well the parties are working together, this can be a satisfactory way of holding down the legal costs. Mediators often recommend this approach.

La Russa Must Know

Regardless of what you decided, remember that life as an attorney isn't as glamorous as some believe. Longtime Cardinals manager, Tony La Russa (a law school graduate), when asked why he never entered the legal profession, replied, "I'd rather ride the buses in the minor leagues than practice law for a living."

CHAPTER 4

Mediation

A Note on ADR

ALTERNATIVE DISPUTE RESOLUTION (ADR) is about solving problems without going to court and having a judge solve them for you. It's neither a new nor a complex idea. When a husband and wife sit at the kitchen table to negotiate their divorce settlement, that's ADR.

Many couples successfully reach an agreement doing just that. And while it's always recommended that the settlement still have some general legal review, no one should argue that they simply didn't spend enough money and suffer enough aggravation to get a good deal. Indeed, the goal of ADR is to save on both, and the breakfast nook often works wonderfully well for doing just that.

Although not all spouses can reach a settlement on their own, many will still see the benefits of avoiding a trial. A variety of ADR techniques have been developed to help them achieve this goal. Today, the most popular of these methods is mediation.

What Mediators Do

Many people confuse arbitration with mediation. Arbitrators hear a case and enter an award that the parties agree in advance will be legally binding. Mediators don't make any rulings or final decisions. Instead, they attempt to get the spouses to work out their own solution. Settlements are never forced upon the parties. This means that mediation may not resolve the problem. But, more often than not, it does lead to a settlement.

The mediator's role is to create an atmosphere that reduces hostility and encourages understanding and compromise. Through the use of probing questions, role playing, and similar techniques, both parties come to better understand the desires of the other, as well as their own central needs. The objective is to reach an agreement that is satisfying to both sides.

Mediation can be particularly helpful when dealing with deeply emotional issues, such as where the children will live, how and when the kids will see each parent and the grandparents, the process for making important decisions regarding schooling, healthcare, religion, etc. However, as well as it works for some folks, it's not for everyone.

This is especially true when there is a major imbalance in the parties' bargaining power due to the intimidation or the mental or physical abuse of one spouse by the other. It also may not work well when one side is regularly abusing alcohol or drugs.

Finally, if one partner is far more sophisticated in terms of financial dealings, negotiating skills, etc., than the other mediation may be less likely to succeed. It depends on the level of trust that exists between the parties, the ability of the mediator, and the amount of support (lawyers, financial advisors, child-development specialists, etc.) that is made available.

Mediation is not counseling or therapy. It tries to get to the inner feelings of the parties only for purposes of reaching a settlement. There is no attempt to make your spouse a better person.

Who's a Mediator

The majority of mediators in Missouri are either lawyers or come with a background in the behavioral sciences (psychology, social work, child development, etc.). As in most of the U.S., Missouri mediators are largely unregulated.

There's no state certification or direct government control placed on mediators. Anyone can print a business card declaring that he or she is a mediator. However, this doesn't mean that there aren't many excellent mediators in the Show-Me State.

In addition to their law or other relevant backgrounds, most mediators take specialized training in mediation and other dispute-resolution methods. Such courses are widely available. The University of Missouri–Columbia, St. Louis University Law School, Missouri State University–Springfield, and Washington University Law School in St. Louis all offer excellent mediation training.

National and state mediation organizations have minimum standards for membership. Knowing that a mediator has met these experience requirements provides a starting point in the selection process. Locally, you can check with the Association of Missouri Mediators (AMM) at www.mediate.com/amm. You'll find it a good source for more information, including a list of members who have at least 40 hours of mediation training.

You can also check with your local Circuit Court to find out what training it requires for mediators. Many circuits publish lists of approved mediators who meet qualifications established by the court.

Picking a Mediator

All good mediators come to the mediation with certain background skills. But rarely will they be expert in all the divorce disciplines (child development, financial analysis, legal rights and responsibilities, etc.), though they will have training in these disciplines.

If the mediation relates to only one specific issue, it makes sense to select a mediator who has a lot of experience in that area. For example, when mediating the distribution of business assets, it's best to find a mediator who understands financial reports. A few hours of training may not be enough.

On the other hand, a different set of skills is required when it comes to children. Mediators who read complicated business documents as easily as we read the *Post-Dispatch* might have much less experience in settlements relating to kids.

A dilemma can arise when a couple wants to mediate a variety of divorce issues. One solution is to get a different mediator for each subject area. But in practice almost always a single mediator is used. Outside experts will often be employed to provide additional technical support during the mediation, while the mediator focuses on the task of facilitating a resolution.

Speaking of experts, if your mediator happens to be a lawyer, don't expect him or her to also act as an attorney for you and your spouse. In fact, a mediation lawyer is specifically prevented from doing that. The reason is that a mediator must remain neutral; a mediator acting as a lawyer would by definition have to advocate for one client or the other (not both). So if you're in need of legal advice and protection, you have to get a separate attorney.

It's a Matter of Style

Another important selection issue is deciding on the style of mediation that will work best for you.

Many mediators feel it's important that the couple develop a settlement on their own. They believe this approach achieves the strongest feeling of "ownership" in the final decision. When the answer comes from the parties themselves and not an outsider, long-term success is far more likely. Using this method, the mediator helps guide the couple into discovering what works best for them, while never making specific recommendations.

But some mediators see their roles differently. They reason that many individuals have little or no experience in solving the problems of divorce. Suggesting alternatives that have worked in other cases is not forcing the couple to accept a solution. Their feeling is that without this assistance the solution developed by the parties may be faulty and not lasting, or that a settlement will never be reached.

Regardless of the philosophy, the key to a successful mediation is that the mediator remains entirely impartial. Other than that, there can be more than one correct approach. What works best in your situation is a matter of personal preference. Get recommendations and interview several mediators. Select the one you and your spouse like best.

Different Strokes for Different Folks

Couples doing a *pro se* divorce (using no lawyer) often rely on a mediator to help them arrive at a complete settlement. When the parties have retained separate lawyers, the use of mediation may be more selective. It depends on how enthusiastically their attorneys embrace the process and the desires of both spouses.

Pro se couples usually come to the mediation session with a reasonable amount of openness and flexibility. Their lack of a preconceived settlement makes it easier to find common ground. The negative side of this is that one or both spouses may be unaware or misinformed about important legal rights. Part of the mediator's responsibility is to ensure that this shortcoming is appropriately addressed.

Just the opposite may be true for couples already working with lawyers. The attorneys will have discussed with them their rights, possible settlement structures, and likely court judgments if things are allowed to go that far. When their clients show up at the mediation, they may have some firm ideas regarding the ultimate resolution.

While knowing your rights is important, a good settlement has to reflect more than what the law grants to each party. It's possible for the spouses to achieve all their "rights" and to still be unhappy with the final outcome. Therefore, the discussion must be approached with sensitivity to the needs of both sides rather than focusing only on each party's legal entitlements.

And don't think of mediation as a one-time event. Many people find it to be a valuable tool for resolving issues at any point during the divorce process (and even after the divorce). So if you don't want to mediate all the divorce issues, use mediation where you think it might work.

Kids and Money

Regardless of the number of issues to be mediated, it's important to separate the child-related issues from the financial issues. Failure to do this can sometimes result in bargaining the kids against the money.

Mediators will make every effort to prevent such a situation from occurring. However, creating a procedural firewall is also helpful. For example, agree not to have any discussions on the financial matters until everything about the children is resolved.

Mediation by Force

Remember when you were small and your parents forced you to play with a visiting cousin? The one who kept kicking you? Well, the court often takes a similar approach.

In certain parts of Missouri (the Kansas City area, to name one) the judge may require that the parties attempt mediation before proceeding to the courtroom. This is especially common with respect to resolving the child-related issues. In fact, all parenting plans (statewide) must include a dispute resolution provision for attempting to settle differences out of court. Mediation is the method usually listed.

In no case will the court demand that the mediation must resolve the issue. It requests only that the couple try. If, after a couple hours of mediation, one side determines it isn't working, the ADR can be ended. But often, unlike the case with your kick-boxing cousin, the parties will find some common ground through the imposed mediation and avoid a trial (at least for the items mediated).

Saving Money in Divorce Is a Relative Concept

One benefit of mediation is that mediators are often cheaper than lawyers. And there has to be only one mediator.

The cost of hiring a mediator normally runs from $100 to $300 an hour. The lower amount is more common for a nonlawyer mediator in rural areas, with the highest often in effect for a lawyer acting as a mediator in St. Louis, Kansas City, and similar locations.

But it isn't only about money. Many people discover that a better, more satisfying settlement is achieved through mediation compared to the confrontational processes of lawyers' letters flying back and forth or fighting it out in court.

Divorce agreements, especially those involving children, are frequently operational for many years. Success is far more likely over the long haul when they are arrived at with the least amount of "bloodshed."

"Peace in Our Time"

However, feeling good about an agreement isn't always the best measurement. In the late 1930s the Prime Minister of England sat down with Hitler and worked out a peace-keeping treaty. While he triumphantly returned to London claiming success, the cataclysmic events of World War II soon proved otherwise. In a somewhat exaggerated fashion this demonstrates a potential pitfall of the mediation process.

The fact that the parties think they've arrived at a good deal doesn't automatically mean that the best conclusions have been reached. Many of us admit to being terrible at negotiating the price of a new automobile. So how do we suddenly gain the wisdom to properly represent ourselves in such an emotional and legally complex event as divorce? The short answer is that these skills don't magically improve.

But talented mediators can prevent a catastrophe. While not specifically directing the composition of the settlement, the mediator is well aware of what makes sense and what is foolish both legally and logically. If one or both of the parties seem to be going off the deep end, the mediator will step in to redirect the effort.

Frequently, these problems come up when there is a lack of accurate specialized information. A single issue may be quickly clarified by having the spouses telephone a lawyer, an accountant, etc. Broader problems may require that these specialists actually attend the mediation.

Having experts participate in the relevant mediation sessions certainly adds some expense, but the alternatives are often less desirable. The lack of critical information on a timely basis can bring a promising discussion to an abrupt halt. Even worse, decisions may be reached that are based on incorrect technical (legal, financial, etc.) assumptions. Later, when the error is uncovered, it's really hard to go back and mediate the issue all over again.

Pro se couples might have no choice but to consult a lawyer or other professional on certain topics. The risk of making a serious mistake is just too great.

A perfect example is the Hannibal mother who was prepared to give everything to her husband (including the house, her share of his pension, and the vacation home) just so he would grant her primary physical custody of the children. The mediator encouraged the woman to consult a lawyer before finalizing the deal. Her attorney quickly pointed out that, in her case, she would get the custody she sought regardless of how the assets were divided.

This mother was not happy to give away a property share that was rightfully hers, but, acting out of fear and a serious lack of legal knowledge, she saw no other choice. The result would have been a financial catastrophe had she not sought out expert advice.

Getting It on Paper

No mediation is legally binding unless both sides agree. But if the goal isn't to reach a joint commitment, it's all just a waste of time. So, hopefully at some point in the mediation a verbal agreement gets put into a document called a "memorandum of understanding."

Frequently, these memoranda are signed by the parties, but not always. It depends on what's being resolved and how the agreement will be used.

If the mediation deals with issues to be agreed to in court documents (settlement agreements are defined in the chapter on Missouri's legal process), it's really not necessary to create a contract during the mediation itself. Later, the settlement agreement (sometimes called a separation agreement) will be signed, and that's certainly a legal commitment. In fact, if the mediator is a lawyer, he or she may produce a separation agreement instead of a memorandum of understanding, and the separation agreement can be used by the court in finalizing the divorce.

However, a good reason to sign all mediation documents is a very practical one. Often when verbal agreements are put into a memorandum for signature one or both of the parties will suddenly get cold feet. If they're still miles apart, it's better to find out sooner than later.

Legal Mumbo Jumbo

An important goal in mediation is to break down the adversarial barriers and create an atmosphere of understanding and trust. That's certainly an effective way to achieve a good resolution. However, once the mediation is over, everyone steps back into the hostile "real world."

Legal commitments resulting from mediation are serious business. So it's important to have a lawyer review the understanding to ensure it meets current standards for fairness and legality and to draft any agreement that is going to be signed.

It may seem like a waste of money to translate a clear commitment between you and your spouse into complicated legal language. But should it become necessary to enforce the contract in court, that procedure will be quicker and less expensive and the outcome more certain if it was written by a lawyer. Besides, people usually live up to a well-drafted agreement that allows little room for interpretation.

Once again, it's important to point out that even if the mediator is a lawyer, he or she doesn't represent your legal interests. A review by an attorney working as a legal expert just for you is the only way to be certain your rights are protected.

Lots of Ways to Skin a Deer

In the end, a blend of methods works best when negotiating with your spouse. Start by sitting down one on one and discussing the situation. Do it in a pleasant, neutral location where you will not be interrupted, preferably not at your in-laws' house.

This is the cheapest and often easiest approach. If help is needed, try mediation. Mediation isn't magic but simply an effective process for putting people in a position to reach a common understanding. It's still up to the divorcing spouses to find that understanding.

Keep your attorney informed if you have one. *Pro se* couples shouldn't be afraid to consult a lawyer occasionally as well. And stay open-minded to all settlement options. Sometimes giving in on something of less value to you than to your partner will deliver back an item you really treasure. Remember, compromise isn't a sign of weakness; it's evidence of intelligence.

CHAPTER 5

Collaborative Divorce

A New ADR Approach

SMART PEOPLE don't want the court to solve their divorce issues. It's expensive, it's time consuming, and it's extremely uncertain. And often these uncertain results are very final. The process also strips away one's privacy and control with respect to the things that people care most about. A trial should be the last option and never the first or even the second.

Yet for some, the kitchen table negotiation goes nowhere. And mediation either doesn't work or isn't right. Starting around 1990 a different twist on alternative dispute resolution (ADR) was introduced, and in the past several years it has begun to gain a lot of interest and success. It's called "Collaborative Practice" or "Collaborative Divorce" (referred to here as CP). CP combines aspects of mediation and legal representation with the assistance of expert support from various disciplines.

Of course, all this high-powered advice doesn't come cheap. Then again, going to court is likely to be more costly, and the result may be considerably disappointing. That's really what CP is all about: maximizing the opportunity to reach a deal giving both sides the most they can (or at least should) hope for in a way that leaves the fewest scars.

Over 90% of divorces are settled without a trial. Nevertheless, so many people view the situation from the wrong end of the binoculars and prepare for court from day one. CP allows the parties to focus all their efforts and resources on finding a settlement rather than on preparing for trial. A trial that has only a 10% chance of ever happening.

Do or Die with Collaborative Practice

There's no mediator used in Collaborative Practice; instead, the sides must have separate lawyers. Before starting, the parties, along with their attorneys, sign a "participation agreement" which states:

- they will deal with each other in good faith
- they will freely exchange all relevant financial information
- they will attempt to settle the case mainly through four-way meetings involving the two clients and two lawyers
- all experts (appraisers, accountants, therapists, etc.) used in the CP process will work in a cooperative effort to resolve the issues and will not be used in a future trial (if CP fails) unless both sides agree
- during the CP process neither side will file any document with the court
- if the case cannot be settled through CP, both lawyers must withdraw and cannot be part of the trial process

All these items are important, but it's the four-way meetings that define the process.

Collaborative Practice four-way meetings are about the two sides working together as one. At these discussions information and ideas are openly exchanged. Everyone is fully committed to finding a settlement. Remember, if CP doesn't work, a new team will have to be assembled to take things to trial. That's the rule and the threat as well.

So What's It Like

Imagine a super-sized kitchen table negotiation. In addition to you and your spouse, there are the constant helpers (the two attorneys). Meanwhile, technical experts come and go as needed. All the information you desire arrives magically on demand. Need legal advice? You've got it. Need to know the value of the house? You've got it. Need some help from a child-development expert? It can all be there.

Adding to this positive experience is the fact that everyone in the room wants only to see the two sides leave with a fair and livable deal. Neither party is posturing or threatening. It's not one spouse's experts versus the others. All the rowers are pulling in the same direction. That's Collaborative Practice.

Can't happen? Better think again about the consequences of failure.

The Details

Once the collaborative attorneys (each representing one side) are chosen, they'll schedule an initial meeting to include the parties and themselves. At this meeting agreement will be reached on what divorce issues have been decided (for example, perhaps both sides already have agreed on some custody issues) and what issues remain to be resolved.

Based on this discussion, an outline of future meetings with specific dates is developed. In addition to listing the topics to be covered, it will indicate what information needs to be provided by each side (bank and business records, income and pension documents, tax papers, report cards, medical records, etc.). If experts must attend the meeting (accountant, child specialist, appraiser, etc.), that also will be part of the plan.

The lawyers generally come to all the meetings, but it isn't always required. If the parents need to spend an hour working with a child specialist to get information on parenting options, it's possible the couple can do that together without their attorneys. Later at a four-way meeting this topic can be reviewed and the decision finalized. A lot depends on how well the two sides are able to cooperate and how comfortable they both feel about the situation.

At some point all the topics get worked out (plan on roughly four to ten two-hour meetings for an average divorce with kids). The lawyers then write up the final settlement, which both parties sign. The rest is a simple process of submitting it to the court for approval. An agreement that is developed in this manner with the close involvement of the lawyers is virtually certain to be accepted by the judge without change.

Maybe by now you're thinking, "Hey, what's the big deal about Collaborative Practice?" While the process sounds like a normal negotiation, it's far from that. The difference is the level of cooperation that takes place between the two sides and the level of available expertise.

Coach Me Up

Another key element of Collaborative Practice is the use of coaches. At the start each party may select a separate coach in the same way as he or she would select a lawyer. Coaches come with certifications as psychologists, marriage and family therapists, social workers, or clinical counselors. They focus on resolving emotional and psychological issues that act as barriers to the couple negotiating the divorce.

For example, if a spouse is simply unable to sit in the same room with the other party, no amount of legal expertise on the part of the lawyers is likely to change that. Yet without the two sides working together, the only solution is to go to trial. It's the job of the coaches to get the couple in a cooperative mental position that will allow the divorce issues to be resolved.

Generally, each coach first meets with his or her client for a separate meeting. This is followed by a four-way meeting (the couple and the two coaches) where agreement is reached on how they will communicate, etc. The importance of this step in the CP process shouldn't be underestimated. It's critical if both sides are to fully cooperate in reaching a final agreement

A list of coaches can be found on the Collaborative Practice websites (listed below) or one can be suggested by your attorney. Charges run in the area of $125 to $200 an hour. In addition to the client meeting and the initial four-way meeting, coaches may also attend other meetings from time to time to address issues that require their expertise.

Arriving at Collaborative Practice

It's not necessary to progress from one-on-one discussions, through mediation, before arriving at Collaborative Practice. CP can be the first choice right from the get-go. What settlement process is chosen has to do with the situation and the nature of the people involved.

If the divorce doesn't involve children or a lot of complicated assets, it makes sense for the couple to just sit down together and get it done. Other simplifying factors include a short marriage where the contributions of the parties are pretty clear and there's no request for maintenance (alimony). In such straightforward cases why go hunting for rabbit with a bazooka? Naturally, both sides have to have a positive attitude about working together to settle things fairly.

Mediation helps a couple get in touch with what is really important to each side and how to structure those feelings into a settlement. However, it potentially presents some problems as well. Perhaps one spouse isn't comfortable negotiating in front of the mediator without his or her attorney or other knowledgeable advisor present. Some might feel a bit overwhelmed by everything and afraid of making a mistake.

Collaborative Practice helps equalize the balance of power between the spouses by having lawyers at the table. This can be especially important in cases where abuse has been alleged. It's also more suitable for complicated cases where technical information (appraisals, child development, legal advice, financial analysis, etc.) is a key element.

Follow the Rules

Just as with mediation, no state laws govern Collaborative Practice. The rules are set up by organizations that are dedicated to seeing CP grow and prosper. Experience has proven that if all the CP rules are followed there's a good chance of success.

Currently, in Missouri three professional associations have been organized by CP practitioners (more are likely to develop): the Collaborative Law Institute (Kansas City), the Collaborative Family Law Association (St. Louis), and the Mid-Missouri Collaborative & Cooperative Law Association, also referred to as the MMCCLA (Columbia and Jefferson City area).

Typical requirements for a lawyer to become a member of these organizations are:

- being a member of the Missouri Bar and having five years of practicing law
- having substantial family law experience (St. Louis requires 40% of a member's legal practice to be family law)
- passing a written test or taking continuing legal education in the area of ADR or family law
- In St. Louis completion of 40 hours of divorce mediation training as well as an eight-hour interdisciplinary collaborative law training course.

Mediation vs. Collaborative Practice

If it isn't clear to you by now, let's summarize the difference between Collaborative Practice and the two most popular other choices, mediation and litigation.

Mediators aren't allowed to represent or express the interests of either of the parties. This certainly includes restrictions on providing legal or financial advice. They simply can't take sides or even look like they're doing so. Many mediators will only facilitate the discussion and never propose anything. This can be a real problem for a spouse who isn't on a level playing field with the other.

Imagine the circumstances of a divorcing Bethany couple. Thomas runs a complex family business, and

Barbara teaches first grade. All day long Tom is negotiating business deals and reviewing financial reports. Meanwhile, Barbara is in a classroom teaching seven-year-olds to read.

It isn't reasonable to expect Barb to single-handedly represent her interests with respect to a business that Tom knows intimately and she barely visits or even to hold her own in a full-blown negotiation on other divorce issues. Barbara needs some help to equalize the balance of power. In a CP divorce her lawyer can advise her and even speak for her at the meetings to more clearly present her perspective and proposals.

Barb's rights may be equal to Tom's, but her ability to express them is not. This isn't an issue of intelligence; it's all about experience and personality.

What About Litigation

Keep in mind that the involvement of attorneys doesn't automatically turn things into a *Boston Legal* event. Finger-waving lawyers, hysterical witnesses, and a gavel-pounding judge may be what the trial-bound crew will experience, but they are hardly on the Collaborative Practice agenda.

That's a key difference between having CP meetings and a courtroom adventure. Trials are adversarial proceedings. The basic concept is for the two sides to go at each other full blast with somehow the correct result being found along the way. Lawyers are trained to do this, and most are good at it. But what's left when the smoke clears?

Such an aggressive environment almost ensures that the relationship between the parties will be further damaged. Especially when kids are involved, this isn't a good thing. After all, the parents will have to raise their children together, perhaps for many years into the future.

Meanwhile, rather than achieving a handcrafted settlement that both parties contributed to (fitting their needs and lifestyle), the court is likely to spit out a cookie-cutter judgment that neither side really wants. Or, if the judge persuades the parties at the last minute, and after weeks of costly trial preparation, to settle the case out of court, it's often very difficult to come up with a thoughtful resolution. What a wasteful approach.

Not to mention that trials and trial records are usually completely public. They are conducted on the court's schedule—not yours. And because the letter of the law must be followed, they are subject to greater delays and many added expenses.

Selecting a Collaborative Lawyer

Most lawyers are trained to represent clients on a one-sided basis. So while going to court isn't what most people (including their attorneys) want, a major segment of the system is designed to do just that.

This makes picking a lawyer for Collaborative Practice a bit more difficult than finding one for a more traditional approach. Many lawyers will be unaware of exactly what CP is (have them read this chapter) or may not be interested in participating or could lack the necessary training.

It's likely that the farther one gets from the geographic centers of the three Missouri CP programs, the more difficult finding a collaborative lawyer will become. None of this means that CP is not a good way to go. It just takes time for word to get around in the rather slow–to–change world of our legal system.

Try the direct avenue and go to the websites of the founding organizations. The Collaborative Law Institute's website (www.collablawmo.com), the one for the Collaborative Family Law Association (www.stlouiscollaborativelaw.com), and the one for the MMCCLA (www.mmccla.org) all provide more information on Collaborative Practice as well as lists of participating attorneys.

Once you get hold of these membership lists the selection process is much the same as that outlined in the chapter on picking a lawyer.

The Check Please!

In the end, each couple must decide what approach best satisfies their requirements. Just remember that the value of anything isn't what you pay; it's what you get for what you pay.

There's no doubt that using no lawyers and no mediator and going completely *pro se* is the most economical method to end a marriage, but it could be a poor value—something that may not become fully apparent until months or years later. Anyway, let's do a rough estimate on what a Collaborative Practice approach is likely to cost.

Start by assuming that between four to ten CP sessions lasting an average of two hours will be required to settle a complete divorce, including the child-related issues. In addition to the attorneys' fees, it's prudent to budget one individual providing professional support (financial advisor, CPA, child specialist, etc.) for each meeting. This expert may sit in on the meeting, or you may need to meet with the expert before or after the session. Other costs, such as appraisals and actuaries, may also be needed, so figure a couple of hours of their time as well.

In addition to the meeting costs there are expenses related to completing the standard divorce paperwork. Of course, because the couple is getting along so well, these charges will be minimized. So add to the time spent in CP sessions another six hours of the attorney's time for each side.

If the lawyers charge $250 an hour, and the experts cost $175 an hour, the rough cost of a two-hour meeting will be $1,350 ($1,000 for two lawyers for two hours plus $350 for an expert for two hours). Using this estimate, the cost for four meetings is $5,400, and for 10 meetings, it's $13,500.

You may also have four-way meetings involving coaches and the couple without the lawyers. These meetings will run around $700 each and it would not be unusual to have anywhere from two to six such meetings.

Now add to this cost $3,000 ($1,500 for each attorney) for the six hours per side needed to prepare and administer the divorce documents (6 hours x $250 per hour x 2 lawyers). Finally, there are likely to be some miscellaneous expenses, so include an extra $500.

The grand total results in a range of between $10,300 (four sessions with attorneys plus two sessions with coaches) and $21,200 (ten sessions with attorneys and six sessions with coaches). That's the total expense for both parties, not for each party. This does not, of course, include the costs of appraisals or other reports generated by outside experts. Keep in mind this is just a ballpark figure. It's possible to find qualified professionals operating either below or above these amounts, and you can adjust the figures based on the actual charges of the people you contact.

Also, some divorces have special issues that can dramatically increase this estimate. Naturally, such special issues would also affect the cost of going to trial (probably by an even greater amount than handling them through Collaborative Practice).

On first blush, most people will think that Collaborative Practice isn't cheap. They're absolutely correct. The good news is that it's much less expensive than going to court. Just ask your friend who went the trial route. And also ask how pleased your friend was with not only the result but also the entire process.

Read a Book

Books that discuss Collaborative Practice in detail can be helpful when trying to determine if it is the best option for you. Two choices on the recommended reading list are:

> *The Collaborative Way to Divorce*, by Stuart G. Webb (inventor of CP) and Ronald D. Ousky

> *Collaborative Divorce*, by Pauline H. Tesler and Peggy Thompson

The Critical Factor

All methods of alternative dispute resolution rely on the parties' working together. Collaborative Practice provides technical and emotional tools that will "backstop" each side. These resources make up for differences in negotiating skills, intellectual and informational resources, and much more. But only one spouse has to have ill will to ruin the game. For nothing leads the parties to the courthouse steps faster than a bad attitude.

In divorce there's usually no shortage of hurt feelings, and trust is a fragile thing. Yet, despite the pain and pressure of the dissolution process, a positive relationship can survive. That is if both sides make a total effort each day to let it. It's definitely in their best interest to try.

Instead of dwelling on the bad old days, look ahead to better times. As Cardinal baseball legend Stan Musial once said of negotiation, "Don't remind them of what you did in the past—tell them what you're going to do in the future."

CHAPTER 6

Legal and Physical Custody

No Kid Poker

MISSOURI'S LEGAL PROCESS operates best when the two sides work cooperatively on the issues involving care of the children. That's the hopeful objective behind ordering the parenting plan. Judges are particularly unhappy when one or both parents attempt to use the kids as bargaining chips.

A Defining Moment

Now on to the subject at hand. Normally, the key to success in approaching a complicated subject like child custody is to have a clear understanding of the terms. However, Missouri challenges that convention. So particularly when it comes to physical custody, don't get too hung up on what things are called. In Missouri "what you see is what you get!" What you call it just isn't as important.

That being said, let's try on a few definitions. The first thing to learn is that there are two major types of custody. Many people think custody is used only to describe where the children will primarily reside, but that's not the whole story.

Legal Custody—This is about how decisions are made. Which parent has responsibility for determining the education, medical and dental care, religion, travel, and any other matter involving the children's welfare and upbringing. What kind of school the children go to (anyone for home schooling?), what sports they can play (football is too dangerous!), what dentist is used (do you believe in holistic healing?) are some of the legal-custody decisions.

How legal custody is awarded usually has little to do with the amount of physical custody granted. It's possible for a parent to have an equal vote regarding the legal custody of the kids and to see them only a few weeks a year. Maybe he or she lives in California or travels all the time.

Physical Custody—This relates to where the children spend time. It's usually defined in terms of so many "overnights" per week/month/year. It can also be allocated in terms of "visits" (something less than overnight time with the children) if that makes more sense. Examples of this might be if an infant is breast feeding or if the visiting parent is unable to house a child on a regular basis. Normally, both parents get some amount of physical custody. It can be divided up equally (50%–50%) or in some other proportion.

The Hard Part

Now let's break these two categories into some subheadings. Most of the following terms are really not well defined (or not defined at all) under Missouri law, but you may still run across them in your lawyer's office, in the courtroom, and even in this book.

Sole and Joint Legal Custody—These terms are defined very clearly. Either both parents can equally share legal custody rights (joint legal custody), or the rights can be awarded to only one side (sole legal custody). See below for more details.

Sole and Joint Physical Custody—These designations sound important, but they actually don't have much effect on the situation. If one parent is given sole physical custody, the other parent will almost always be given "rights" to temporary physical custody. The word "temporary" means that the physical custody is only part of the time, with the rest going to the parent with sole physical custody. It doesn't mean that the right will disappear or expire in the future.

The law fails to specify the number of nights that must be awarded to each parent in order for the judge to call it joint physical custody. In the end, whether physical custody is shared jointly or one parent is given sole physical custody and the other gets temporary physical custody rights makes little difference. A parent has full authority regarding the physical custody of the kids while they are in that parent's care. Your focus should be on how much time you get to see the kids and not what it's called.

Primary Physical Custody—If a lawyer mentions "primary physical custody," be sure to ask what he or she is talking about, since that term doesn't appear in any Missouri law. Nevertheless, it's often used, and many dissolution judgments include the phrase.

One reason it keeps getting used is that sole physical custody sounds so harsh. In general, primary physical custody, or primary custody, refers to a situation where the children spend substantially more of their time with one parent than with the other.

Residential Parent—Even when parents equally share joint physical custody, one of their homes must be designated as the mailing address for the children and the address used for educational purposes. The person whose address is assigned for this purpose is sometimes called the "residential parent." This is another term that doesn't appear in the law books.

Certainly, if one parent gets more of the overnights than the other, it's likely that he or she will be the residential parent. Beyond indicating the percentage of overnights, this designation has virtually nothing to do with a parent's physical-custody rights.

Visitation—While the term "visitation" is found in Missouri law, it has no clear definition. Everyday people think that it refers to the time the child stays with the parent not getting physical custody, but this isn't usually correct. Normally, both parents get some percentage of physical custody, and the word "visitation" doesn't come up.

However, judges sometimes award visitation rather than physical custody to one spouse. This seems to happen more often when the number of overnights being specified is small. Meanwhile, Missouri law in some sections confusingly refers to the physical-custody schedule as visitation. Yikes!

There's really no practical difference between visitation and physical custody. So, as suggested earlier, just keep your focus on what the best schedule is for your kids.

Splitting the Babies

Here's one more possibility to consider. Parents don't always have the same amount of physical custody with all their children. Under a split-custody ruling, one side takes primary responsibility for the physical care of some of the children, with the other parent having more time with the rest.

The split-custody route is never high on any judge's list of preferences. After all, divorce is hard enough on a family without dividing up the siblings as well. However, split custody will be ordered if that's what both parents want and the situation looks like it makes sense for the kids.

It can also be ordered even if only one parent requests it and the judge feels it's in the best interest of the children. Or the judge can come up with the idea independently. Regardless of the method, split custody isn't a common occurrence.

First Stop, the Parenting Plan

Okay, now that the terminology and some of the realities have been explained, here's how it actually works. Everything begins with the parenting plan.

Both parents must submit a formal parenting plan within 30 days following the service of process (meaning the date the summons is delivered to the respondent) or the filing of the entry of appearance (meaning when a lawyer lets the court know he or she is representing the respondent). The plan covers all dependent children under 19 years old. The parents can do it separately or together.

Parenting plans explain how physical and legal custody are to be handled, including the schedule that both parents will use to see the children. It can also discuss specific issues of religion, schools, etc.

But the plan doesn't have to be limited to just the legal requirements. It can specify who pays for private school, daycare, college, the wedding, Olympic training, and anything else the parties come up with.

Parenting plan forms are available from your Circuit
Court, or go to the website of the Office of State Courts
Administrator (www.courts.mo.gov) and look under
Publications. However, every family is unique. Don't
hesitate to adjust these forms to better reflect your situa-
tion. Cookie-cutter parenting often doesn't work.

The Temporary Order, Maybe

If the parents agreed to a single parenting plan, the judge
almost always assumes it's in the best interest of the
child and goes along with the deal. In this situation,
unless one side requests it , no temporary order (also
called a *pendente lite* or PDL order) will be issued. The
document is just filed with the court, and both parents
live up to it.

When two separate parenting plans are submitted, it's
up to the court to decide. This often requires a hearing
for temporary orders (a PDL hearing). Understandably,
judges hate trying the case twice. After all, temporary
orders last only until the final judgment (frequently just
a few months).

That's why some jurisdictions will order parents to seek
mediation if they're unable to reach agreement on a single parenting plan. Other circuits have social workers
available to help matters along. Ask your lawyer or the
circuit clerk for details.

In the end, a smart couple will agree on one parenting
plan. After all, who can be certain what the judge will
decide? A judge doesn't know your children or care
about your children the way you do. So a parent unwilling to compromise with the reasonable requests of the
other party may end up with the court granting him or
her even less. It happens all the time!

Finally, the court cannot enforce a parenting plan unless it's part of a temporary order. Therefore, if you suspect your spouse may fail to follow the agreement, consider requesting the judge to issue a "consent PDL." Unlike a regular PDL where the court decides on the parenting plan, with a consent PDL the court simply takes the plan agreed to by the parents and makes it an order that is enforceable, if necessary, by the court.

Temporary Tends to be Permanent

Now that you've decided to cooperate, here's a word of caution.

Don't be misled by the term "temporary" when applied to the initial physical and legal custody ordered by the court. These decisions create a framework for the final order that's sometimes difficult to change once in place.

Consider, for example, a father who agrees to his wife's taking care of the children most of the time while he sees them on weekends only. If that situation continues for months while the couple prepares for trial, he will have a much tougher time convincing a judge at trial that he should permanently have the kids in his care 50% of the time. It would be much easier if he had insisted on a temporary plan that gave him the kids half the time right from the start.

Yet this initial stage is also an opportunity for the two sides to try a cooperative approach. The parenting plan is worked out shortly after the divorce filing, and tempers can be hot. This may not be the best environment to make lasting decisions regarding such emotional issues.

It all gets down to just being practical. Don't agree to a temporary structure you honestly believe will be a disaster. But go forward with trying a reasonable one, even if

you have some doubts. The judge will usually appreci-
ate this cooperative effort and remain flexible regarding
the final arrangement.

Frequently, by the final hearing the spouses will have
fine-tuned things into a plan that works for everyone. If
not, there's nothing to stop them from battling it out at
the trial. Just remember, one parent is going to lose that
battle, and even the "winner" may be unsatisfied.

The Times, They Are A-Changin'

And who knows if anyone will be pleased in the future.
That's because things like the overnights allocation
don't automatically adjust as the child gets older. If the
divorce involves a four-month-old baby the judge may
order a custody schedule appropriate for that age,
including, for example, the youngster's breastfeeding
requirements.

It will remain unchanged when the kid is 18 years old
unless a parent goes back to court and requests some
alteration. So, assuming the child is very young, it's possible that, over the years, the issue will be back in court
several times.

The best way around this problem is to work out the
future ahead of time. It's easy to foresee that an infant
who can't be separated from either parent for more than
a day or two will be far more able to handle longer
absences by age five. Cooperating parents can build
such predictable changes into the parenting plan.

Regardless, it's impossible to anticipate everything that
might occur 10 or 15 years ahead. As unexpected devel-
opments pop up, it's sure a lot simpler and less expensive when the parents work additional adjustments out
between themselves rather than running to court. Just

make sure significant changes are filed with the court so they're enforceable. This is relatively easy to do and not very expensive if both sides are in agreement.

Eight Magic Factors

Has anyone out there missed the importance of the two sides agreeing on a single parenting plan and then working cooperatively in the future? An aid in accomplishing this objective is to understand how the court goes about deciding custody if the parties can't agree. This knowledge helps to keep the negotiations firmly attached to the real world.

In Missouri the judge must consider the following eight factors—each item will be specifically addressed in the final judgment. The law doesn't indicate any order of importance, but everything isn't equal. The guiding principle is determining what's in the best interest of the children.

> 1. *The wishes of the child's parents as to legal and physical custody and the proposed parenting plan submitted by both parties.*

Like St. Louisan Redd Foxx use to say on *Sanford and Son*, "This is the big one!" Redd was talking about his heart, and factor one truly gets to the heart of the matter. Believe it or not, the judge enjoys giving parents what they ask for. So if both sides work together on a solid proposal, they are likely to get it. On the other hand, if one or both of the parties submit plans that are selfish and unreasonable, the court will take note of that too. First impressions can be lasting ones.

> 2. *The needs of the child for a frequent, continuing and meaningful relationship with both parents and the ability and willingness of parents to actively perform their functions as mother and father for the needs of the child.*

Kids need regular contact with their mother and father, so the judge will work to maximize this interaction. Just because one party lives in California while the other is in Missouri doesn't mean the court isn't going to try to find a way to keep that West Coast parent involved. Of course, the parents have to be willing to participate.

3. *The interaction and interrelationship of the child with parents, siblings, and any other person who may significantly affect the child's best interests.*

This is about knowing who the important people are in a child's life and designing a plan that works to maintain these relationships. The idea is to minimize the amount of destructive change. The custody ruling should hold together as much of the good stuff as possible, rather than tearing things further apart. In particular, the court will determine who has been the "primary caregiver" to the child during the marriage. That parent is likely to wind up with a greater amount of physical custody.

4. *Which parent is more likely to allow the child frequent, continuing and meaningful contact with the other parent?*

The court has no interest in giving responsibility to someone who attempts to destroy the child's relationship with the other parent. This is often reflected (good or bad) in the parenting plans (if separate ones are offered), as well as the overall impression each parent makes on the court. A parent who refuses reasonable requests by the other parent for time with the children is likely to be penalized.

5. *The child's adjustment to the child's home, school, and community.*

How positively integrated into the current situation is the child? If he or she enjoys the current living arrangement, is involved in many local activities, has lots of friends, and is performing well in school, the court will be eager to maintain such a happy state of affairs.

6. *The mental and physical health of all individuals involved, including any history of abuse of any individuals involved. If the court finds that a pattern of domestic violence has occurred, and, if the court also finds that awarding custody to the abusive parent is in the best interest of the child, then the court shall enter written findings of fact and conclusions of law. Custody rights shall be ordered in a manner that best protects the child and any other child or children for whom the parent has custodial visitation rights, and the parent or other family or household member who is the victim of domestic violence from any further harm.*

Wow, that's a mouthful. And how can an abusive parent be in the best interest of the child? Well, it depends if the domestic violence was directed at the child or at the other parent. Regardless, the court is required to make a clear explanation (both logical and legal) as to why it decides to give custody to the abusive parent. This is something that a judge does only after giving it a lot of thought. Don't go into the courtroom thinking that being an abusive parent will not be held against you.

7. *The intention of either parent to relocate the principal residence of the child.*

If giving custody to one of the parties means that the children will have to start a new life many miles away from important relationships, that is a major change. How will it affect the star goal keeper when he or she has to leave the local soccer team? The same goes for trading a home and favorite horse in Prairie Hill for condo life and a goldfish in the New Jersey suburbs.

8. The wishes of a child as to the child's custodian.

Not every state takes into account what the kids want. Even in Missouri the answer to this question is applied carefully. The desires of a five-year-old may not be given much weight. He or she can't possibly understand the entire situation. But what a 15- or 16-year-old wants may be more important. It's often a matter of, "If all other things are relatively equal, what does the child prefer?" But be careful before hauling your kids into court to testify. Judges don't like this and often think that a parent who brings a child in to testify can't be doing what is in the youngster's best interest.

And the Answer Is...

It doesn't take a rocket scientist to address the above eight factors. The fact is that both parents normally love their kids, want the best for them, and provide as much attention as possible.

But in most families parenting chores are not equally shared for a variety of practical reasons. This makes the spouse doing most of the caregiving (the primary caregiver) easy to spot and more often than not his or her home becomes the children's principal residence.

For many years moms were virtually always given primary physical custody. Lately, that has changed somewhat (the trend is toward joint physical custody), but not as much as you may think. Mothers still get primary physical custody most of the time because they're usually the main caregivers, not just because they're the moms.

Even so, if you haven't been doing the majority of the parenting, it may not be too late to take a shot at getting primary physical custody. The trick is to convince the judge that following the divorce some big changes are going to take place for both parties.

That's because the stay-at-home parent who spent end-less daytime hours nurturing the kids during the marriage will now be working too. He or she will have no more time to spend with the kids than you will. Maybe less, depending on the situation. So the playing field will start to level out.

This story goes over a lot better with the court if during the marriage you spent a large dose of your after-work hours actively with the children. If it's a matter of "I'll do better in the future," your chances are greatly reduced.

Getting What You Wish For

But before doing anything, make sure you want and are able to perform the responsibilities of the primary care-giver.

Are you ready to attend all the parent–teacher conferences, drive the kids to the doctor and dentist, stay home when they're sick, do their laundry and their shopping, attend the school concerts and all their other activities, put them to bed, bathe them, cook for them, comfort and discipline them, etc?

Forget about fighting to get primary physical custody just so you can "stick it" to the other side. If the other parent is better positioned to take the lead role in physical custody, let him or her have it. Maybe you'll get a dividend in another area.

Practical Physical Custody

The number one thing most parents want to know is how the court will divide up the overnights. After all, it's possible for the parent with temporary physical custody to get the kids up to 50% of the time.

But first, take a blank calendar and fill in a few months, showing the average time you spent each day with the kids during the marriage. Surprise!

Not even married parents have 100% physical custody, and most don't have even 50%. Indeed, does anyone really want to spend all their time with the kids? No nights bowling, no Saturdays golfing, and no evenings shopping without the children. Kids need time off too, just as much as they need to regularly experience the love of both parents.

And because divorce brings on a number of lifestyle changes, try doing the calendar exercise for a few months into the future as well. Even from a selfish standpoint giving the other side ample physical custody is usually a good deal.

Of course, if there are issues of abuse or poor character (drugs, neglect, etc.) with the other parent, it's an entirely different situation. But that's the exception. Too many people view their percentage of physical custody as a measurement of their parental qualifications or as a victory over the other parent. That's nonsense.

Some also believe that achieving more overnights provides a financial benefit in terms of the child-support burden. The real truth is that the parent with most of the money is going to pay the most regardless of the custody decision.

So, forget any unhelpful ideas you may have and work towards an arrangement that is practical and rewarding for both sides.

Deciding the Overnights

Now with your feet planted firmly in reality, let's look at what influences the overnights decision.

The first consideration is the age of the child. Not so long ago, psychologists were saying that toddlers must have stable surroundings (avoid shuttling back and forth) and recommended only limited overnights with the parent having temporary physical custody. Today the feeling is quite different.

Now most child psychologists believe the parent–child bonding process is largely completed by age two. This means that before that date, it's important for both parents to spend a lot of time with the youngster. It also means that after two years such constant contact is less important.

Of course, this doesn't mean the parent without primary physical custody should see less of a child if the young-ster is over two, but it does allow other factors (distance, expense, activities, etc.) to have more influence on the overnights decision.

Naturally, the distance the two parents live from each other represents a practical limitation. Kids need to attend one school all year, stay in touch with their friends, and keep up with extracurricular activities.

So if the non-residential parent is beyond school-com-muting distance, then overnights during the week are probably out. When the distance is really great, time and cost restrictions can limit weekend and monthly visits as well.

Legal Custody Reality Check

Just as with physical custody, it's important to be realis-tic when it comes to the legal custody decision.

If the child is eight or ten years old, many of the most important decisions have already been made. The doc-tors, schools, sports, etc., were largely chosen before the divorce. What are the chances that a parent given sole legal custody will suddenly abandon the kids' religion and join a "Kool Aid sect" down in South America?

And when the youngsters reach their teens, you had better be willing to compromise anyway—not with the other parent, but with the kids themselves.

Normally, the court's inclination is to grant joint legal custody. However, if the judge gets the impression that every consultation between the parents is going to be a World War III scenario, then sole legal custody will be the preferred choice.

However, the best way for the couple to protect themselves from future surprises is for the parenting plan (discussed earlier in this and the divorce-process chapter) to set forth all the important items that concern the couple (the doctor to use, the school to go to, the religion to practice, etc.). Then regardless of a sole or joint legal custody situation, both sides will get what they want. Or at least what they agreed to.

Of course, there may be major exceptions to the argument that legal custody issues are often more limited than many fear. But choose your battles wisely. If you rarely had disagreements regarding such matters during the marriage, try to keep it all in perspective and don't worry too much.

Compromise or Else!

Parents can avoid the unwanted court battles over custody issues before and after the divorce through mediation or Collaborative Divorce (see relevant chapters). However, these approaches require the willingness of the parents to reach some kind of compromise.

When the relationship between the parties is likely to remain in a high-conflict state after the divorce, the judge, if the couple agrees, may incude a "parenting coordination order" in the final judgment (it must be in the final judgment to be required later on). The parenting coordination process is usually able to resolve the thorniest problems without having to go to lawyers and deal with busy court dockets.

So if it's in the final order, then each time an unresolved custody issue arises following the divorce, the parenting coordination process gets implemented. It starts with a mediation-style investigation and negotiation headed by a parenting coordinator (a mediator, psychologist, social worker, lawyer etc.) selected by the parties or by the judge. The coordinator contacts the parents, together or separately, in person or by telephone, to review the disputed child-related issues. The opinions of teachers, counselors, therapists, etc., may be solicited. Older children may also be interviewed.

Through this process an attempt is made to resolve the problem. However, if the parents can't reach a consensus, then the parenting coordinator decides for them and that decision becomes legally binding immediately. Thus, unlike with mediation or Collaborative Practice, it's possible for the coordinator to act as a final arbitrator if all else fails.

Parenting coordination is faster and more effective than repeated trips to court and deals with issues that judges would just as soon avoid. Costs run between $150 and $300 an hour (occasionally more), with the higher fees usually for lawyers acting as coordinators. Hopefully, the result is more satisfying for all involved. Especially for the kids.

A Call to Arms!

Unfortunately, not everyone is willing to put the good of their children above their own self-interest. There is nothing meaner in the entire divorce process than an all-out custody battle. In its worst form, this is not merely a nasty litigation, it's a nuclear war, a total suspension of reason and decency. Like Godzilla meeting a junkyard dog.

While not often used, either spouse can request, and sometimes the court on its own will demand, that a forensic evaluation be undertaken. A psychologist is called in to methodically interview the parents and children along with friends, neighbors, school counselors, any therapists working with the kids, etc. In addition, each family member undergoes psychological testing, either written or oral, depending on the individual's age.

The study requires four to eight weeks to complete and costs between $3,000 and $7,500. Normally, the parties share the expense. In the end, the approximately 25-page report boils down everything into recommendations regarding legal and physical custody.

You can expect a psychological evaluation to say something good and bad about each parent, and you can also predict that any parent who takes exception to the evaluator's conclusions is going to hire another expert to refute those findings. Get out your wallet!

But even without a forensic evaluation, both lawyers will be working overtime preparing for the trial. A parade of expert witnesses may have to be called in as well. Every skeleton in every closet is dragged out for display. You will recall that divorce trials are open to the public along with most of the court documents. Think about that.

All this is expensive. A first-class custody battle can run $50,000 per side or more. Keep in mind that this figure doesn't include the other divorce issues. It's not surprising that such warfare tends to increase in proportion to the client's ability to pay. Yet, even when money is limited it's easy for costs to get out of control as emotions overwhelm good sense. It's time for everyone to calm down, at least a little.

Kids Have Rights Too

If the adults are determined to fight over custody or child support, the judge may feel the need to protect the children's rights and appoint a guardian *ad litem*.

A guardian *ad litem* is an attorney who acts as the legal representative of the children (although not, technically, the kids' lawyer). He or she makes recommendations to the judge regarding what is in the best interest of the kids. These recommendations reflect the independent judgment of the guardian *ad litem*, based on interviews with the children (if they are of appropriate ages) and other individuals having knowledge of the children (relatives, teachers, scout leaders, doctors, etc.).

Fees and expenses for the guardian *ad litem* are paid by one or both of the parties based on the judge's decision. When there's no money available, the state may pay, but that's not the usual case. So if the parents can't compromise on custody and child support, they may end up paying for three lawyers (one for each of them and one for their children).

Unlike some states, Missouri allows children to express their desires regarding who should get primary physical custody, the number of overnights, etc. This includes possibly testifying in court. When the kids are asked to participate in such a manner, the court may appoint a guardian *ad litem*.

Such testimony is normally given in the judge's chambers with the lawyers, but not the parents, present. The testimony is sealed, and no one may discuss what was said with the parents. All this is done so the child doesn't worry that what he or she says will get back to the parties. However, it's not a perfect system and if the final divorce judgment is appealed, the possibility exists that the child's testimony would become known to the parents.

A guardian *ad litem* must be appointed when child abuse or neglect is being alleged.

Missouri, Love It or Leave It

Everything in this chapter is based on the divorce taking place in Missouri. But what happens if the children have been moved or are scheduled to move out of the state?

To begin with, in virtually all cases a parent is prohibited from moving the kids out of the location where they lived during the 60 days prior to the date the divorce petition was filed. The only exceptions are if the court specifically approves such a move or the written consent of the other parent is obtained. Any violation of this requirement is likely to be punished quite harshly by the judge both directly and possibly in the terms of the final divorce order.

However, it's a different situation with moves made more than 60 days before the divorce petition is filed. That's because Missouri law provides both parents with equal rights to the kids during the marriage. Either party can do what he or she wishes as long as there's no court order stating otherwise. But does anyone want the children to get caught up in a tug of war across state lines?

Shopping for Your Court

Putting aside that emotional aspect, moving out of Missouri prior to the divorce filing can put into question where the divorce should take place. Courts, not only the ones in Missouri, don't like a "forum shopper" (a parent who moves to another state in order to get under a friendlier jurisdiction). Judges will also give the relocating spouse a hard time if the move was made to make it difficult for the other parent to see the kids.

This doesn't mean that it's impossible to move from Missouri. Just make sure it's for a good reason, such as the mom who can't afford to stay in the marital home and so she moves in with her out-of-state parents. Or one of the parties may need the emotional support of distant family members and friends.

In the end, if the kids haven't lived in a state for at least six months, that state will rarely hear the case. However, if a spouse and the kids have lived outside of Missouri for a long enough period, there's a good chance that the divorce can be handled in the new state. In that situation, you'll need to buy a different book!

A final point is that you can't forum shop within Missouri either. If the kids have been moved to a different circuit court district within 90 days of the divorce being filed, the other parent can get the case returned to the original circuit.

Moving After the Divorce

That's pretty clear, but what about after the divorce is final? Often a parent's objective in seeking sole physical custody is to be able to relocate the kids in the future. Or just the opposite: he or she wants to ensure the youngsters can't be moved away. It's very dificult to move a significant distance away from the other parent without consent. Courts frown on it.

At one time the parent with primary physical custody had much more authority to change locations, but no longer. Restrictions go way beyond questioning moves from South Lee to South America or even just to South Dakota.

Missouri law requires that before either parent relocates the children, the other parent must be given 60 days advance written notice by certified mail. If the parent with temporary physical custody doesn't agree to the move, the only alternative is to see whether the court can be convinced.

That's easier said than done. A judge is very reluctant to overrule the objections of the dissenting parent.

Consider the primary physical-custody parent in Gilmore with a job offer increasing his $62,000 salary to $85,000 (a 22% increase). The hiccup is that he needs to move to Kansas City.

His former wife, also a Gilmorian, isn't so enthusiastic. So he runs to court, explaining the logical benefits behind moving west (money, future job growth, bigger house for the kids, etc.).

Most likely the judge will tell the promoted parent that he should stay in his current position and learn to love Gilmore more. If the moving parent insists, it's quite possible that he will no longer have primary physical custody.

The same goes for a Natural Bridge Junction mother with primary physical custody. Having found Cody, the man of her dreams, in Kyle (not so far away), she plans on marrying him and moving into his home with the kids. If her former husband objects, Cody is likely to be riding the range in NBJ and not Kyle.

But a relocating parent with only temporary physical custody also raises concerns. Moving could easily reduce that parent's physical custody rights as well. Don't forget, the kids have to get to school from both houses. Or there may be no time and money to deal with the kids' traveling back and forth to the new location on weekends, etc.

Of course, if the nonresidential parent lives across the country and physical custody involves a week at Christmas and four weeks in the summer, moving from LA to San Diego may not have much impact on the situation. Just remember that any change potentially puts everything regarding custody schedules into the hopper again. The possible results can be uncertain.

This uncertainty drives home the value of maintaining a good relationship with your spouse during and after the divorce. Maybe the two of you can find a solution that works for both sides.

Speaking of solutions, it's not unusual for one or both parents to change addresses immediately following the divorce. This needs to be settled though negotiation or by the judge as part of the final judgment. If there's a negotiated agreement, make sure any planned address change is put in writing and filed with the court. The same is true for relocation agreements reached after the divorce.

Remember, the very big no-no is moving without either the other parent's agreement or the court's permission. A relocation that takes place without such approval could result in a dramatic change in the physical-custody rights of the wayward parent.

Fair and Square

Some parents also make big mistakes in other areas of the custody process.

A woman from Green Ridge was determined to get sole physical and legal custody of her child. Actually, there was no doubt that the kid would be staying with her the majority of the time, but the husband wanted to share the decision making (legal custody).

In order to prevent this from happening she accused the husband of molesting the child. Even though the father proved he was innocent, it became difficult for him to touch his daughter for fear of his actions' being misinterpreted.

Making this kind of false accusation can result in the judge awarding sole custody of the children to the injured party, even when the accusing parent would normally have received it. There is simply no justification for using such deceptive tactics.

In difficult divorces like the preceding one, it's important to keep a diary covering your spouse, the kids, and the divorce in general. Make it simple. Purchase a calendar that you use exclusively for your divorce, and write the daily events in the boxes provided for each day. The divorce process may take up to a year (occasionally longer), and it's hard to remember exactly when each thing happened or how often.

Caution, Judge Ahead!

Generally people don't know much about judges. Yet many parents willingly place their most valuable possessions (their children) in the hands of these perfect strangers.

Don't be misled by TV series, novels, Bill O'Reilly, and congressional investigations. Judges are just as different from each other as normal people are different from each other. Some like doing family law, and others are happy to move on as soon as the opportunity arises.

The law is often not an exact science. Judges' views on parenting reflect their personal and professional experiences. They want to do what's best for the children, but they're not experts on child development. How will your judge think? No one really knows.

One thing for sure is that no judge loves your children the way you do and, hopefully, your spouse does. Why then turn the controls over to someone who didn't even know your kids' names a few days ago?

The comedy M*A*S*H* talked about doing "meatball surgery," and often our courts could say the same. Parents want to use scalpels when making the delicate decisions, but judges don't have that luxury and are stuck with chainsaws instead.

A Word to the Wise

While many aspects of a divorce are a one-time deal, raising the children (whether the parents are married or divorced) is a long-term joint project. It doesn't take any great intelligence to realize that the parents, assuming good intentions on both sides, will be able to work out a better plan than the court. If you need some help, try using mediation or the Collaborative Practice process (see the related chapters).

Keep your attorney updated on the negotiations. This will allow you to stay informed of the rights and obligations both parents have under the law. And make sure a lawyer reviews all agreements before you sign them. Once they're signed, it's difficult to go back requesting changes because you didn't understand the deal or you forgot to include an item.

Finally, even if you know that the court will give you the kids and decide most issues in your favor, try to reach a balanced agreement with your spouse instead. A court-imposed custody decision that you love and your spouse hates will come back to haunt you and your children.

CHAPTER 7

Child Support

Before We Begin

THROUGHOUT THIS CHAPTER and in other portions of the book the phrases "primary physical custody," "custodial parent," and variations of these expressions are used. Even though such terms don't appear in Missouri's dissolution laws, they are frequently employed as shorthand by lawyers and judges to refer to the parent having the children in his or her care for more time than the other parent.

Since readers aren't training to become attorneys, the feeling was to use references that aid in the understanding of the topic despite not representing a correct legal term. Those inclined to attempt the bar exam should keep this fine point in mind.

Don't Wait to Be Asked

Things are often in motion even before the divorce filing takes place. Frequently one spouse has moved out of the house, while the other spouse stays at home with the kids and becomes the de facto parent with primary physical custody—at least on a temporary basis.

Under these circumstances, for the "moved-out spouse" to make voluntary child support payments is just smart thinking. After all, it's pretty clear what the children's needs are and the amount of money each parent is able to pay.

Doing so reduces the pressure on the parent with the kids who is suddenly facing the physical and financial demands of raising the family alone. Everyone has a chance to catch their breath while getting emotions under control. Sometimes, in this improved environment, an attempt can be made to reconcile the marriage. Even when that's not possible, certainly a better atmosphere for negotiating a settlement is established.

A PDL, Maybe

In Missouri a child support order is always in the final judgment. But if the parties just can't agree on things while going through the dissolution process, a temporary child support order can be requested as part of the PDL (also called a *pendente lite* order or temporary order). It will remain in place until the final order is issued. (See the discussion on *pendente lite* in the chapter covering Missouri's divorce process.)

So once the divorce petition is filed, if your better half isn't sharing the cost of the youngsters, you need to hurry on down to the courthouse and seek a PDL order specifying temporary child support. Each court has a different procedure for obtaining a temporary order, and it may be a few weeks or even months before one is issued.

Some reluctant spouses think that delaying child support payments will save them money. That's not necessarily true. Depending on how the judge views the circumstances, payments may be ordered retroactive to the filing date of the divorce. Anyway, the judge has a lot of opportunities to penalize poor behavior in the final divorce order.

Yet delays often arise when the primary physical custody parent asks for too much money or one spouse is trying to punish the other or the noncontributing parent is acting foolishly.

The Paying Parent

In Missouri only one parent pays child support. Ingeniously, the court refers to him or her as "the parent paying support," while the other party is called "the parent receiving support." You may think that rarely are legal terms so understandably descriptive. But wait, it's not quite as simple as that.

Child support is not paid to the kids. It's paid to the parent with primary physical custody or the parent with the lower income if the parents share equal time with the children. While only one parent makes child support payments, both parents have financial responsibilities to the children.

Does it make any sense for the receiving parent to write a check to him- or herself each month? No, but both parents are expected to contribute to the financial support of the youngsters in proportion to their incomes.

Child Support Guidelines

The child support guidelines incorporate the tables and worksheet calculations judges rely upon for determining who will be the paying parent and the amount to be paid.

The guidelines are the responsibility of a special committee appointed by the Missouri Supreme Court. They are periodically revised in order to reflect the rising cost of living. As explained in the chapter on Missouri's divorce process, their purpose is to ensure that the minimum needs of the children are met on a uniform basis across the state.

That being said, parents don't have to follow the guidelines. For example, based on a couple's circumstances, the guidelines may say that the paying parent needs to provide $600 in monthly support. Yet the parties can decide to reduce that amount to only $300 a month (maybe in exchange for a commitment on some other issue). This will usually be fine with the judge as long as both sides agree. If they can't agree, expect the judge to impose the guideline amounts.

Welcome Aboard Form 14

Even if the parents (in separate plans or in one they agree on) use a child support amount that's different from the guideline figure, they must calculate the guideline amount by filling in a worksheet called a Form 14. The completed Form 14 is provided to the court at the time they hand in the parenting plan.

Completing Form 14 is no *Love Boat* cruise. It's more like traveling on the *African Queen*. The first sign of trouble is the more than 20 pages of instructions. Of course, if you consider doing your taxes with a two-dollar calculator to be a recreational activity, then it's full steam ahead. For the rest there are some lifeboats on the horizon.

A helpful one is the availability of computer programs used to prepare the form (kind of a *Turbo Tax* for divorce). Just type "MO Form 14" into a favorite Internet search engine and make your software purchase.

Another approach is to hire someone to prepare the worksheet for you. This will normally be a lawyer who has the expertise to make sure things are done correctly and as much to your advantage as legally possible. A lot is on the line and mistakes can be costly.

But no matter how you choose to do it, some important issues have to be resolved first. The key ones are parental income, spousal support (alimony), physical custody, daycare expenses, and medical insurance. Let's discuss them one at a time. After that we'll get into the details. If you're reading this late at night, you may want to hold off until the morning. It's a little complex.

Calculating Parental Income

Okay, here we go. The first thing you have to fill in on Form 14 is the individual incomes of the parents. It's essential that the total income is established to ensure that the court order (if the parents are unable to reach agreement on their own) is within the couple's ability to pay. It also allows the court and the lawyers to calculate the percentage of the total income that each parent brings to the table.

For example, let's say one parent has a $7,500 monthly income and the other parent earns $2,500 monthly. The table of basic child support obligations (Form 14) can then be used to calculate the amount the parents should be spending on their children.

Assuming this amount is $1,500 a month, the child support obligation of the parent earning $7,500 a month will be 75% of the child-rearing costs, or $1,125. That's because $7,500 is 75% of $10,000, which is the combined income of the parents. The lower-paid parent's obligation will be the remaining 25% ($375).

It's not always so easy to come up with each parent's income. Missouri has its own way of calculating how much you earn (or should earn or could earn). In many cases the income reported to the IRS is merely a starting point.

Since income affects several other divorce issues in addition to child support, a separate chapter has been dedicated to the income discussion. However, let's review one key item here.

The court expects that everyone should work. If a parent doesn't work, there needs to be a good reason. Usually, the judge will accept the custodial parent remaining home with a preschool or disabled child. However, if the kids are all in school and everyone is healthy, the assumption is that both parents need to earn a living.

Therefore, the court will want to determine a nonworking parent's job prospects. To assist the judge in this evaluation, the working parent is likely to provide testimony from a vocational expert witness regarding the kind of employment the nonworking spouse is qualified for and the likely salary. The nonworking spouse may provide an alternative view.

Once the court decides on the proper income assumption, the nonworking parent's child support contribution will be calculated using Form 14. The fact that the parent is not actually working and currently has no income normally doesn't matter to the court.

Consider the paying parent who earns $6,000 a month while the court finds that the non-working parent with primary physical custody should be able to find employment and make $4,000 a month. So their combined income could potentially be $10,000, of which the paying parent's earnings would represent 60% ($6,000 is 60% of $10,000).

If the child support requirement for the children totals $2,000 a month, the paying parent has to pay only $1,200 a month ($1,200 is 60% of $2,000). The nonworking parent either gets a job in order to provide the missing $800 or manages things on the $1,200.

Income and Spousal Support, Etc.

If a parent is paying or receiving court ordered maintenance (alimony), that also gets listed on Form 14. The income of the parent paying the maintenance is reduced by the full amount of the maintenance payment. At the same time, a spouse receiving this spousal-support payment has to add it to his or her income.

For example, if you're receiving, or will receive, $1,000 a month in maintenance (from a past or current marriage), add $1,000 to your monthly gross income on Form 14. If your current spouse is making that payment to you (or to his or her ex-), he or she gets to deduct $1,000 per month.

Court imposed obligations to pay child support for children not from the current marriage, regardless of where the children reside, are also shown on Form 14 and get deducted from the relevant parent's income before using the guidelines.

Who's Got the Children

Now that the income issue is pretty much settled, let's move on to the impact of physical custody.

In order to finalize the Form 14 calculation, the parent with primary physical custody and the amount of time the kids will spend with each parent have to be determined. That's because the receiving parent (the one getting the child support payment) is almost always the one with primary physical custody of the children. And the number of overnights each parent has affects the payment amount.

The parents can make these decisions for the judge in a jointly agreed-to parenting plan and avoid the topic coming up at a PDL hearing. There's no need for a PDL hearing to get temporary orders if the parents agree on all the temporary issues. At most, only a brief hearing is required down the road to complete the divorce if they can agree on all the items permanently.

Assuming the parents leave it up to the court, the primary custodial parent is usually the spouse who performed the major caregiving activities during the marriage. Even if the parents share physical custody 50–50 following the divorce (an equal number of overnights), one parent will normally have responsibility for making the major educational, medical (possibly including insurance), recreational, and general living purchases for the youngsters. The paying parent will be the one to assist with these costs by making a child support payment.

The Visitation Effect

How overnights are determined should the judge be left to decide was discussed in the chapter on legal and physical custody. Now let's spend a moment to discuss how overnights affect the child support calculation.

Well, as the paying parent's overnights go up, that parent's child support payment tends to be reduced. This reduction reflects the fact that to the extent the children are spending a greater amount of time with the paying parent, the child rearing costs (meals, entertainment, etc.) paid for by the custodial parent are reduced. So as mentioned earlier, before the support payment can be decided, the overnights schedule needs to be set.

But first an important note. If one parent gets the kids fewer than 36 overnights annually, skip over the rest of this discussion. That's less than 10% of the year and just isn't significant enough for the court to make any adjustments.

It's a different story when the annual overnights are 36 or more. In that case the court takes the child rearing expenses determined on Form 14 and applies the following reduction to the amount due from the paying parent:

Annual Overnights	Percent of Year	Reduction
36 to 72	10% to less than 20%	6%
73 to 91	20% to less than 25%	9%
91 to 109	25% to less than 30%	10%
110 or more	30% or more	up to 34% (varies with the judge)

For example, let's say that before taking into account the visitation effect, the total child rearing cost for the children is calculated on Form 14 to be $1,500 per month and of that amount the paying parent has to pay 60%. If the paying parent has a visitation schedule of 85 overnights a year, the preceding chart provides for a 9% payment reduction.

So first calculate 60% of $1,500 ($900), and then reduce that number by 9% of the total $1,500 child rearing expense (9% of $1,500 is $135). The paying parent's monthly payment will be $900 minus the $135 adjustment, or $765.

So Why Isn't It Less or Maybe More

You may be wondering why the adjustment is so little. After all, 85 days represents 23% of the year. Shouldn't the adjustment be about 23% instead of only 9%? Not the way Missouri figures things, and it does make some sense.

The state separates child rearing costs into the following three categories:

1. *Variable*—38% of child rearing costs are directly dependent upon the amount of time each parent spends with the kids (things such as food, recreation, transportation).

2. *Duplicated Fixed Expenditures*—30% of child rearing costs are not directly dependent on the overnights schedule. A good example of this is housing. Both parents need to have a place for the kids to stay, regardless of whether they come every week or once a month. Of course, if the children visit a lot, maybe a bigger home, etc., is required.

3. *Non-duplicated Fixed Expenditures*—32% of child rearing costs are not dependent on the overnights schedule at all and also don't need to be duplicated by both parents (these would include clothing, school supplies, music lessons, etc.). Usually, these costs are paid for by the parent with primary physical custody.

If the number of overnights is more than 35 and less than 110 days (between 10% and than 29% of the year), the court takes into account only variable costs (see the above definition) when making adjustments. Therefore, in the case discussed earlier, the 9% adjustment reflects only the higher variable costs experienced by the paying parent. Duplicated and nonduplicated expenses are not considered.

When the overnights exceed 109 days, the court will begin to consider the duplicated fixed expenses incurred by the paying parent. However, there is no universal formula to do this and the judge is left to consider the specifics of the case. Usually, these reductions can be anywhere up to 34%. If overnights are shared 50–50 generally, there is a 34% reduction. But, if it's anything less than 50–50, 10% is the number you'll see most frequently.

What about Daycare and Medical Insurance

Daycare can also have a big impact on the amount of child support paid. However, it must be qualified day-care. That's the kind needed so the parent receiving child support can work or attend school (for approved work-skill training). It's got nothing to do with hiring a babysitter for a Friday night out with the boys or girls.

Qualified daycare costs increase the total child support figure dollar for dollar. For example, take the situation of a stay-at-home mom (a receiving parent) with two kids. The guidelines may come up with a total child rearing cost (including the receiving parent's responsibility) totaling $1,500 a month. However, if the mother decides to work and pays $500 a month for daycare, the required child support figure goes up to $2,000 ($1,500 plus $500).

But we're not done yet. If the receiving parent is entitled to a federal daycare tax credit, that credit must be sub-tracted from the total daycare expense before the daycare expense is used in the child support calculation (this is true even if the spouse, for whatever reason, doesn't actually take the tax credit). Only the remaining amount is added to the child support figure.

In the above example, if the mom can get an annual day-care tax credit of $1,200 ($100 a month), the total monthly child-care requirement will go up only to $1,900 ($1,500 plus the $500 daycare expense minus the $100 tax credit).

Medical insurance is handled in a similar manner. The out-of-pocket cost a spouse pays (doesn't include the portion an employer may pay) for medical insurance specifically covering the children is added to the child support figure.

An example of this would be a paying parent who lists himself and the divorcing couple's two children on his company's medical plan. Assume that the cost of adding the kids to the plan is $140 a month, that the child support amount before the medical insurance adjustment is $2,000 a month, and, finally, that the parents have equal incomes.

In this case the total child support figure would be increased to $2,140 ($2,000 plus $140). The paying parent's monthly support payment would total $930 (50% of $2,140 equals $1,070, from which is subtracted $140 representing credit for making 100% of the insurance payment).

There's a place on Form 14 to enter all this information. It's not a separate calculation. Of course, another approach is to lay it all out in the parenting plan by indicating the percentage (or specific dollar amount) each parent will pay. Since both sides agree, the judge will usually go along.

Taking a Look at Split Custody

If you're undaunted by the confusion generated so far, let's take a look at the effect of split custody on the support calculation. Possibly you will recall from the previous chapter that split custody is when each parent has primary physical custody of one or more, but not all, of the children. For example, Mom gets the girls and Dad gets the boys.

In split-custody cases, separate Form 14s are filled out covering the youngsters in the primary physical custody of each parent. The result will be two child support payments, one to be received by each parent covering the kids in their care. The smaller of these calculations is subtracted from the larger one and the difference is paid by the parent with the greater obligation.

So, for example, suppose it works out that the dad should get $500 a month in child support from the mom, and the mom should get $800 a month from the dad. The the judge simply orders the former husband to pay the mom $300 ($800 minus $500). The mom pays nothing to the dad.

Varying from the Guidelines

As mentioned earlier, the parents can mutually agree to a child support payment that differs from the guidelines. This flexibility carries over to the court if the couple can't agree between themselves. Judges have the power to find that the guideline amount is unjust or inappropriate in a particular case.

Let's say the children's standard of living prior to the divorce was above average. The guidelines may not provide enough money to maintain that standard. If the court believes the paying parent can afford a higher level of support, the judge may order payments above the guideline amount.

Of course, if neither parent is capable of funding the prior standard of living, the payments will probably stay within the guidelines. All family members simply have to make a downward lifestyle adjustment. This happens all the time. The court's intention is not to have one spouse enjoying a mansion while the other lives in a camper.

Generally speaking, the guidelines do a good job of covering the variables, including unusual medical, educational, travel, and other expenses that reflect real world situations that always differ from family to family. In the end, judges like to stick to the guidelines.

The Trouble with Kindness

Most paying parents have good hearts and want to be generous. Nevertheless, there are important reasons why it makes sense for them to be cautious, as well.

At the beginning of the divorce process there are often many one-time expenses. To cover these extra items the paying spouse may agree to make temporary child support payments above the guidelines. At the same time, he or she is unable to commit to this higher support level on a forever basis.

However, a Missouri judge could interpret the higher temporary payments as a reflection of both the children's long-term needs and the paying parent's ability to pay. Rather than using the guidelines to determine the amount of permanent child support, the judge may simply make the generous temporary arrangement part of the final judgment.

While the judge carefully calculates and assigns the child support amount during the divorce, the state of Missouri pays little attention to how the money is eventually used. The court simply assumes that it was spent on the kids.

Meanwhile, a paying parent loses all control over how the money is spent once it's paid as child support. Perhaps the receiving parent believes a trip to Vegas with a lover is a better use of the funds.

Yes, the court can demand an accounting (and some paying spouses will request one), but it's rarely done. The difficulty is that child support doesn't cover only expenses easily traced to a child's needs (clothing, school supplies, doctor bills). It also goes toward family transportation, mortgage payments, utilities, insurance, vacations, etc.

Think about it. When you go grocery shopping, you don't buy one bag for yourself, one for your spouse, and one for the kids. You just buy groceries.

The easiest way for the spouse paying child support to minimize such an unhappy situation is to limit the voluntary (pre-court-ordered) child support payment to the amount set out by the guidelines. If additional money is required from time to time, it can always be "unofficially" provided to the other parent or directly to the kids. Call it a Christmas, birthday, or Truman Day gift, or anything else. Just don't call it child support (or spousal support).

Also, keeping part of the support payment voluntary rather than agreeing to an amount substantially above the guidelines can prevent things from getting out of hand. If cash-flow problems crop up later on, those higher payments (a legal obligation) could become very difficult to make.

Doing the Deed

Is anyone out there still following all this? You're not alone if Form 14 has become a bit intimidating. In fact, if you think it's easy, you haven't been paying attention.

There are other issues that can affect the final support calculation, but the above items are the major ones.

Remember that the parents have to provide a completed Form 14 at the time they supply their parenting plan to the court. If the couple submits separate parenting plans, each will complete a Form 14 based on the custody structure and all the other assumptions shown in their individual plans.

If the judge isn't able to persuade the couple to adopt a single parenting plan, the court will come up with a Form 14 based on temporary orders (the PDL). Until the divorce is final, the payments specified in the PDL will be enforced.

Should the parties leave it up to the judge to decide the permanent child support amount then a new Form 14 will be filled out at the time of the final judgment. It will reflect the permanent physical custody arrangements, spousal support (if any), the resulting final parental income calculation, etc.

Adjusting the Child Support Payment After the Divorce Is Final

Unlike some other parts of the divorce order, the court is very willing to adjust the child support amount as time goes by. However, you can't nickel and dime the privilege.

If the guidelines were used to determine the current child support amount, judges will be most receptive to cases where at least a 20% change (up or down) from the original chart-calculated figure is alleged to have occurred. If the child support figure didn't rely on the guidelines (for example, if the two sides negotiated the amount), then the 20% limitation isn't an issue. In that case, the side seeking the alteration simply has to prove that a substantial and continuing change (up or down) has occurred in either the amount needed or in one or both of the parents' income.

Such changes are common if the divorce involves young children, since payments will be continuing for many years. During that time cost-of-living increases could exceed the 20% threshold.

Also, the income of the parents can fluctuate. Remember, the percentage one parent's income is of the total income of the two parents is a key factor in determining the child support payment.

To understand how this works, consider a couple from Black Jack whose combined annual income at the time of the divorce is $100,000, with each parent making $50,000 a year (50% of the total). Using Form 14, they calculate the child rearing costs to be $2,000 a month. Since the dad is the paying spouse, he sends $1,000 a month (50% of $2,000) in child support to mom.

Later on, Mom graduates from night law school and now earns $60,000 a year (lawyers get less than you think, sometimes). The dad hasn't done nearly as well. He's gone backward and is making only $40,000 per year.

While the couple continues to have a combined income of $100,000, Dad's earnings now represent only 40% of that total. Assuming there's no change in the $2,000 a month child rearing costs, a judge is likely to reduce dad's monthly child support payment to $800 a month (40% of $2,000). That's a 20% reduction. Mom still does not pay anything; she just gets less from Dad.

Unemployment is another reason one parent's income may head south. But this is viewed as a temporary situation. In Missouri there's no mechanism for temporary reductions in child support. The law requires that the change be substantial and continuing. The best approach for temporary issues is to try to negotiate something with the other parent and find a new job fast.

One sure way for child support payments to decline is to have fewer minor kids, that is to say, fewer kids young enough to still require support (see "When Does It All End" below). The final judgment (assuming an alternative isn't provided for in the parenting plan) will usually allow for a reduction in child support as the youngsters come of age.

So if the divorcing couple has three minor children at the time of the divorce, the court will use the guidelines to calculate a child support amount to be paid during the period when there are three minor children, when there are two minor children, and when there is only one minor child. But it isn't just a matter of multiplying the rate for one youngster by two and three. In fact, while the amount of support decreases as the number of kids decreases, the amount of support per kid actually goes up.

For example, the child support amount for three youngsters may be $1,600 a month, but for two children it's $1,300 a month, and for one it's $900 a month. That's because the law recognizes that there's a "start up" cost for raising children, but the cost doesn't double when you have a second or triple when you have a third.

Other opportunities for seeking adjustments (assuming they didn't exist at the time of the divorce) include events that significantly increase the child rearing expenses. If a child becomes chronically ill or handicapped, the cost of long-term medical and related support can be enormous. Perhaps a youngster takes on an expensive extracurricular activity like training for the Olympics or membership in a traveling ice hockey team. A very common situation is one where a parent has moved far away and suddenly the cost of visitation (flying the children from coast to coast) skyrockets (although, if you're the one who wants to move, be prepared to pay).

Finally, until the child support order is modified, the paying parent must continue to send checks in the amount currently ordered. There are serious consequences if these payments fail to be made (discussed below). Anyway, changes the court makes are often retroactive to the date the modification request was first filed.

The Sword and the Shield

It's amazing how Missouri's population grows only a little over 1% a year, yet people seem to be having kids left and right. The ink hardly dries on the final divorce order before one or both of the newly freed spouses are out creating another family (in or out of wedlock). Sometimes it happens before the final order!

If a parent has additional children following the divorce, this added demand on his or her income is taken into consideration by the court when determining whether that parent can afford an increase in child support payments where the receiving parent requests it. The new kids are "shielding" the parent from payment increases.

However, the additional expense of these new children cannot be used as a reason to get existing child support payments reduced. So the added youngsters can't act as a "sword" to slash the already existing payment.

The Money, Please

Missouri doesn't like people who fail to pay child support. The laws are strict and well enforced. A paying parent who isn't paying can be brought to court by the other parent under a contempt action.

If the overdue amount exceeds $5,000, the state provides free legal assistance not only to help collect it but also to possibly send the "deadbeat parent" to jail. Should the back payments exceed $10,000, the poorly paying parent can risk having his or her parental rights terminated.

There are ways to help prevent things from getting out of hand. The parent receiving child support is automatically entitled to wage withholding as a part of the support order unless the parents initially agree otherwise.

Such a withholding order is sent to the paying parent's employer instructing the employer to withhold the child support amount and send it directly to the Family Support Center. This state agency will then transfer it on to the receiving parent.

Doing things this way actually benefits both sides. First, it ensures that the payments get to where they're needed. Second, since the state agency records the payments, the paying parent can never be wrongly accused of failing to pay. Under state law, an employer cannot use wage withholding as a reason to terminate or not hire someone.

And don't forget, paying parents must notify the court of any change of employment or address.

When Does It All End

If the children are very young, be prepared for child support payments to continue for a while. In fact, Show-Me State laws extend the obligation to provide support longer than some other states do.

The basic requirement is for the payments to go on until the child reaches 18 or graduates from high school, whichever comes last, but never past age 21. If he or she goes on to college, the support requirement will end at graduation or upon turning 21, whichever comes first. However, regardless of age or school status, it can be extended further if a disability is involved.

To be classified as "attending college" a child must sign up for 12 credit hours of course work each semester (excluding the summer) and pass six of those hours. A student who works at least 15 hours a week has to carry only 9 credits a semester (the law isn't clear if any of these hours have to be passed). In either case the child must attend continuously and provide evidence of enrollment and grades to the paying parent.

A student who isn't enrolled in school on a continual basis except for summers (no time off between high school and college or between college semesters) or who fails to pass the required credit hours can find the child support terminated by the court. Once terminated it can't be reinstated.

Child support can end sooner if a teenager establishes a separate residence away from the custodial parent. However, before you stop making payments, be sure the court issues a specific order stating that the child is "emancipated" (meaning he or she is legally free from parental control). Emancipation will also occur when a child marries or joins the armed services.

This doesn't mean that a youngster living away at boarding school is emancipated. As long as the parents are legally obligated to take care of a child, the mandated child support will continue.

College Support Order

The substantial cost of sending children to college isn't provided for under the child support guidelines. That doesn't mean the court won't consider adding a college-support requirement in the final judgment if things get to trial. The closer the kids are to college age, the more likely the judge will go along with such a request from the receiving parent. It's also possible to ask the court to modify the original child support order later on as college time approaches.

College-support orders are frequently referred to as "Echele orders" (rhymes with "freckle"). They cover tuition, fees, and books, along with room and board. The standard used to determine these costs is usually the amount charged by beloved Mizzou (the University of Missouri at Columbia).

Since the guidelines aren't involved, the judge is left to figure how much each parent will pay. Decisions can vary a lot.

If one parent is paying child support the judge may apply a good portion of that payment (up to 100%) to the student's dormitory expenses. But in the end, the party with most of the money can expect to pay for the greater percentage of the college costs.

All this uncertainty makes it wise for the parties to negotiate a reasonable out-of-court compromise at the time of the divorce. This might include a deal whereby child support payments are suspended (abated) for a child during the period that child is attending college. In exchange, the paying parent picks up the bill for the higher education.

How to Save a Lot of Money

It's pretty clear that raising a child after the divorce is often a long-term project. Many changes are going to take place over the years. One solution is to fight over every new issue in court. This becomes a very profitable business for the attorneys. A smarter approach would be to review the situation with your former spouse on a regular basis. When changes are necessary, decide on these adjustments out of court.

But remember, any significant alteration agreed to by the parties needs to be submitted to the court. The judge will then issue a modification to the child support order. This will allow the court to enforce these changes in the future if necessary.

Let's take a look at a Pevely couple to see how this works (or doesn't work). The court issued an order for Walter to pay Dorothy, his ex-wife, $900 a month in child support for their son, Daniel. Shortly after the divorce Walt is laid off, and Dorothy verbally agrees to accept a reduced support payment of $500 a month (a $400 reduction).

Twelve months later Walter is reemployed and back earning his prior salary. He offers to start paying the full $900 again, but Dotty says that's not good enough. She goes to court demanding a year's worth of the shortfall in Danny's support payments ($400 a month for 12 months).

Since the original support order had never been officially modified by the court, a judge will force Walter to make up the difference between what he paid during his unemployed period ($500 a month) and what the court order says he should have paid ($900 a month). That's $4,800! And, adding insult to injury, the court will also make him pay interest covering the period of delay at a heart-stopping 12% per annum.

If Walter had gotten the order modified at the time Dorothy agreed to the temporary reduction, this problem would have been avoided. When both sides are in agreement, getting the court to issue such a modification is not time consuming or expensive.

In summary, the money saved on lawyers by a couple working things out between themselves is far better spent on the children. And don't you think the youngsters know that too?

CHAPTER 8

The Status of Children

What's This All About

THIS IS A BOOK ABOUT the divorce process. But it's worthwhile to understand what the situation is for kids born out of wedlock as well. In the upside-down world of "modern lifestyles," it's common for families to include kids from several different marriages, live together romances, and one-night stands.

The status of these youngsters has an impact on two critical responsibilities. The first has to do with assigning legal and physical custody rights. The second is the amount of child support ordered and who pays it.

In a divorce involving children the resolution of the custody issues is built into the divorce process. When the parents are not married, a separate paternity action must be filed with the court. The documents to do this can be obtained from the clerk at the Circuit Court or from a lawyer.

Some of this discussion is covered in other parts of the book. However, it's really important and worth visiting again.

Who's Your Daddy

Everything starts at the beginning. The first step in sorting out the children is determining who are and who are not the parents. This is usually done by having both parties (in either a divorce, live-together split up, or one-night stand situation) stipulate to the court that they are indeed the parents (natural or adoptive). If the divorce involves kids from prior relationships, the stipulation indicates which children are the legal responsibilities of only one of the spouses.

Alternatively, the father can sign an affidavit at the time the child is born and have his name appear on the birth certificate. This will establish the presumption on the part of the court that he is the parent.

But, if paternity is being disputed, then it's time for science to step in and settle the issue. In the old days a blood test was used to identify the mom and dad. However, that test often left room for uncertainty. Today, DNA testing is the preferred method.

Testing DNA samples from both spouses and the children will leave no doubt in a Missouri court as to who the parents are. And you can't refuse to contribute a DNA sample when the judge orders it.

It's Now or Never

This is the time to bring up a sensitive subject. Sometimes a child is born to a married couple and the husband suspects that he is not the biological father.

This feeling can exist for years during the marriage without requiring any action. However, a decision point is reached at the time of the divorce. If the husband doesn't raise this issue and request a DNA test, he will be deemed by the court to be the father.

Once the husband is presumed to be the father, there is
no going back. If a few years or even only a few months
later someone else is discovered to be the father, it's too
late. The husband will not be released from his child
support obligations. So if there are any doubts, the time
to express them is during the divorce/paternity
process.

In some cases the husband has no doubts, but nevertheless down the road finds out he isn't the father. Again,
it's too late to change things. The same is true for live-
together and one-night stand couples. In all cases, once
the parentage order is issued by the judge, it cannot be
reversed. The court's goal is to create stability and finality in the life of the child.

Our Little Babies

Now, let's start with the most straightforward situation:
children for whom both the divorcing spouses are the
legal parents.

In this case, the court handling the divorce will do all it
can to ensure that these kids have a stable home life,
maintain a reasonable standard of living, and get the
benefit of both parents remaining in their lives.

In other words, both parents have a chance to get legal
and physical custody. And they both have an obligation
to support the children, based on their ability to pay.

Everything discussed under the child custody and support chapters applies to these youngsters.

The Other Little Ones

Then there are the children parented by only one of the
spouses. These one-spouse children (stepchildren)
might be living full time with the divorcing couple or

perhaps only part-time (spending the rest of the time with their other parent). The other parent may or may not be providing child support. Perhaps the other parent is dead.

Regardless, the spouse without a legal tie to the stepchildren has no child support obligation after the divorce. For example, suppose the only children in the family of a divorcing couple were parented by the husband during a former marriage. Following the current divorce his most recent former wife (not legally related to the children) isn't required to pay child support.

Also, this stepmother will have no custody rights (including no right to communicate with the children) even if she acted as the primary caregiver during the marriage.

It goes without saying that the wife's parents who acted like grandparents also get nothing. But grandparents have limited rights regardless (see the chapter on grandparental rights).

The Brady Bunch

Things become more complicated if the divorcing family contains kids from earlier marriages (or out-of-wedlock situations) as well as from the current, soon to be ended, union.

In this case the court focuses first on the children who were jointly parented by the divorcing couple. In general, things proceed as if the other kids didn't exist.

Primary physical custody of these jointly produced children normally goes to the parent who was the primary caregiver. All the other custody issues are settled as described elsewhere in this book.

But there are a few additional twists. When the judge looks at each spouse's ability to pay child support, consideration will be given to the fact that one or both parents have additional children from prior relationships to support as well.

For example, a Sedalia couple has two children (Marty and Buzz) from their present marriage and the wife has two more (Kathy and Sheri) from a prior marriage. The judge handling this current divorce will consider only Marty and Buzz when determining the child support requirement.

However, the judge will reduce the wife's earnings on Form 14 (see the child support chapter) by the amount of any child support payments she makes for Kathy and Sheri, the children from her earlier marriage. If she doesn't receive support, the court will deduct from her income what she should spend on those kids. On the other hand, child support she receives from a previous husband isn't added to her income (spousal support payments she receives are added). This could have a significant effect on her share of the calculated support amount.

Missouri Abandons No Child

It may seem as if the court is abandoning the children who are not the joint product of the marriage. Nothing could be further from the truth. The judge is simply sorting out responsibilities. Children of a prior marriage should already be funded under the child support order from that earlier divorce.

Only parents can be required to pay child support. If there's no second legal parent (or he or she can't be found) and money is scarce, it becomes an issue for the welfare agencies. They ensure that all Missouri children receive the necessary basics.

Children Out of Wedlock

In paternity actions (live-together and one-night stands) the children are dealt with much the same as in a divorce. However, there are a few differences.

Although the law is written in a way that doesn't give preference to a mother or father, and even though the "tender-years presumption" (the idea that a young child should be with his or her mother) has been eliminated from Missouri law, the unmarried mother of a toddler is still a bit more likely to be awarded primary physical custody than would a divorcing woman (in both cases mothers with toddlers are more likely to get primary physical custody then the fathers are).

But if the out-of-wedlock kids are older, both parents have an equal opportunity to gain primary physical custody. As in a divorce, the decision will be based on all the factors set forth in the statute: who is the primary caregiver, the parents' wishes, the cooperativeness of each of the parents, intent to relocate, mental and physical health of the parents and children, the children's wishes, etc. Regardless of the court's decision, barring very unusual circumstances, both parents will be entitled to a schedule of overnights in keeping with the best interests of the child.

Legal custody rights (decision-making authority) also get assigned as in a divorce. Grandparents have the same limited rights in the case of out-of-wedlock situations as they do during a divorce.

The child support guidelines for out-of-wedlock kids are identical to those employed during a divorce, as is the method for determining how much each parent will pay.

One last point. In a paternity case, until a decision is made by the court or an agreement is made between the parents, the mother will be primarily responsible for the children. This isn't always the case in a divorce.

As Time Goes By

If a child is a toddler at the time of the divorce or paternity action, the judge may grant the parent without primary physical custody a schedule of overnights that reflects the child's young age. Despite the fact that kids eventually grow up, this initial schedule does not automatically adjust as the youngster develops. Instead, periodic requests must be made to the court to get it amended.

The best way to avoid this problem is for the parents to agree in advance upon a custody scheme that changes as a child gets older. This can be provided to the court as part of the parenting plan.

Third-Party Custody

It should be pretty clear that the parents are by far the first in line to receive custody following a divorce. However, if both parents are unable (significant mental disability or illness, deceased, etc.) or unfit (drugs, abusers, etc.) or unwilling to accept this responsibility, any person can petition the court for custody of the children.

Normally, relatives are next in line, but under special circumstances nonrelatives can have an equal or better chance. Anyone seeking custody must become a party to the divorce. Although the circuit clerk may be able to provide basic information on how to do this, it's a complicated issue, especially if other individuals are also seeking custody. In such a case, having a lawyer will be very helpful.

Children vs. Chevrolets

So far we have been talking about the law. But the statutes cannot cover everything.

Kids are not automobiles. There has to be more to the procedure than checking out their registrations and moving them from one garage to another. Children enter into private contracts with their parents, stepparents, and any adult who cares for them. These are not a legal kind of agreement, they are the human kind.

In all aspects of ending a marriage or other adult relationship, the recommended approach is to settle things outside the courthouse. But, if this advice is going to be followed only one time, it should be when resolving issues related to the care and support of the kids. Whether someone is their legal parent doesn't really matter.

No child should wake up one day to discover that the person he or she depends on for guidance, nurturing and support is suddenly off limits. Nor should the child learn that this individual couldn't care less about seeing or supporting him or her ever again. The obligations of providing care to children frequently extend well beyond the law and go directly to the heart.

The court is very restricted in what it can do in this regard, however. It's up to the adults to do the right thing and work out an agreement that is best for the kids.

CHAPTER 9

Grandparental Rights

Banning Grandma and Grandpa

W HEN A DIVORCE is in the works, grandparents often worry about losing contact with their grandchildren. Tensions can mount if the parent maintaining the primary home for the kids is looking to get rid of "those in-laws." Sometimes it's not only the in-laws who worry. Grandparents might not get along too well with their own children.

As harsh as it sounds, there may be good reasons to keep the grandparents away. Suppose they are abusive or do drugs or drink too much. Perhaps, they endorse a lifestyle that goes against what the parents are trying to instill in the children.

Just because people are older doesn't mean they're automatically wiser. On the other hand, restricting the grandparents could mean that one or both of the parents are simply petty, vengeful, and self-centered.

The Meaning of Visitation

Before going further, let's take a moment to clarify the meaning of the term "visitation," which is used in this chapter to describe the rights that may be granted to the grandparents.

As stated in the chapter on custody, visitation has no specific definition under Missouri law. However, it's most often used when referring to limited physical custody rights. In the case of grandparents, these rights might be as little as the ability to send letters and e-mails to the kids or as much as allowing occasional overnights.

Parents Know Best

Although grandparental restrictions can pop up while the couple is married, a pending divorce often brings simmering bad blood to a boil. Issues that were tolerated during a marriage to keep peace in the family are no longer acceptable. It doesn't matter who's at fault. The divorcing parents are reorganizing their lives, and that may put the grandparents onto a very rocky road.

The big bump in that turnpike is called "parental preference" and it ties right into the court's goal of looking out for the youngsters first. The simple logic behind parental preference is that parents usually know what's best for their children. At least that's what the court believes.

Still, things are not entirely hopeless. Remember the primary rule that will guide the judge: "All actions taken must be in the best interest of the children."

Grandparents are immediately going to claim that keeping them off limits is surely not in the best interest of the children. Maybe so, but winning that legal argument isn't easy. In Missouri, like everywhere else, the judge will be very reluctant to overrule parental preference.

If the grandparents spent little time with their grandchildren during the marriage, it's unlikely that the court will consider their plea for visitation rights after the divorce.

On the other hand, children often live with their grandparents for weeks or months while the divorce process is under way. During these periods important stabilizing relationships develop. Similar bonding can occur if the grandparents provided regular daycare support while the parents worked. If this is the case, the grandparents have a much better chance of winning some "rights."

Permission vs. Rights

But what exactly is a right? Well, let's start off by explaining what a right isn't.

When a parent allows the grandparents to see the children, a grandparental right is not being granted. The parent is merely giving them permission to do so. A right is enforceable by the court. Permission is controlled by someone who has a right (normally the parents or guardian).

Most grandparents don't have visitation rights but instead rely on permission. Parents, whether married or divorced, in most cases happily grant this permission. In return, they gain the assistance and support that grandparents usually provide in great quantity (including free babysitting).

When the couple gets divorced, the final judgment will specify how and when each parent can be with the children. During his or her specified time a parent generally has 100% control over whether the grandparents have permission to interact with the kids.

The only way for one parent to block the other parent from granting such permission is by showing the court that the grandparents represent a danger to the children. Assuming the grandparents aren't Bonnie and Clyde, this permission can allow for a lot of grandparental interaction.

The Divine Little Miss "L"

Let's take a look at a precocious nine-year-old named Lisa who lives in Festus with Kathryn, her mother. Lisa's father, Mark, lives nearby. His physical custody rights include overnights totaling two weekdays each week, every other weekend, and four weeks during the summer. But Kathy has a "thing" about Mark's parents, Joe and June (J & J), and doesn't want them to see little Miss "L."

There's a lot Mark might do to help out J & J. To begin with, he can have his parents visit with Lisa at his home during his overnight periods. There's also nothing to stop him from bringing Lisa during these overnights to his parents' house to visit or even to spend the night. And when Mark runs late at work and asks Joe to pick up the little girl at Kathryn's home for the scheduled overnights, can Kathryn stop him? Nope.

In fact, if Mark leaves town for a few weeks, he might ask J & J to fill in for him. They can pick up Lisa at Kathy's house and take her to their home and return her when the visitation time is over. Mark doesn't have to be around. And as long as he agrees, J & J can take little Miss "L" to Disney World during one of the four weeks Mark has her in the summer.

When the Trouble Begins

Okay, so far so good; but what if Mark dies? Joe and June want only to exchange e-mails with Lisa, but Kathryn forbids it. No e-mails, no overnights, and definitely no Disney World.

As you can see from this example, the trouble usually begins when the parent who favors the grandparents is no longer in the picture. This can be due not only to death but also to several other reasons. Maybe Mark loses his own right to see the youngster (drugs, abuse, etc.), or perhaps he just doesn't care.

If Mark thinks Lisa is an anchor around his neck, he might not seek custody for himself and couldn't care less whether his parents see the child. One day Mark takes off and fails to leave a forwarding address. J & J could wait a long time before he gets around to giving them permission for anything.

Clearly, there's a big difference between having a right and having permission. If Mark's parents had visitation rights, they wouldn't need anyone's permission to see the child.

The Big Court Speaks Up

But the truth is that in many states getting grandparental rights is hardly an automatic thing. In fact, more often than not the parents (married or divorced) have almost complete power to decide with whom the children can associate.

Even the U.S. Supreme Court, which is usually reluctant to get involved in family law matters, did just that some years ago. In a majority opinion, Justice O'Connor confirmed the sanctity of the family unit (parents and children) and the Court's desire to protect this family unit from the intrusion of the state (all 50 plus the federal government) and the grandparents.

This underscores the limited rights that grandparents have. It also suggests that some rights granted to them by state legislatures and state courts might not be constitutional.

Missouri Takes a Liberal Position!

Cautiously undaunted by Justice O'Connor's words, Missouri continues to provide grandparents with the power to seek visitation rights over the parents' objections under the following limited situations:

1. If the parents of the child have filed for divorce

2. If one parent is deceased and the surviving parent denies reasonable visitation rights to the parent of the deceased parent

3. If a grandparent has been unreasonably denied visitation with the child for more than 90 days (this argument is not valid if the natural parents of the child are still married to each other and are living together with the child)

4. If a child is adopted by a stepparent, another grandparent, or other blood relative

Maternal and paternal grandparents have an equal ability to seek this visitation. It doesn't matter if the parents of the child are not currently married or were never married.

Get It in the Court Order

Just don't start believing that because someone fits into one of the four above categories gaining visitation is a sure thing, because it isn't. Grandparents should never start with the idea of going to court. A trial is their last resort.

So if the divorcing parents aren't completely in agreement with respect to all the grandparents seeing the children, an attempt should be made to negotiate a deal privately, or through some kind of mediation. Frequently, much more can be gained in this manner than by slugging things out before a judge. Remember, parental preference is a significant obstacle to overcome in court.

Make sure that whatever negotiated agreement is reached with the parents gets included in the final judgment. Putting it in this document transforms the grandparents' permission to see the kids into their right to see them. Later on, these rights can be enforced by the court should it become necessary.

And don't forget to cover the little details. For example, some families have a reunion every few years that the kids need to attend, or the grandparents want the children to be at extended family weddings. They may want to be able to contact the school to find out how the kids are doing and to attend athletic and other events involving the children. Many wish to send Christmas and birthday gifts, exchange letters, e-mails, and pictures. And don't forget Disney World.

Would anyone deny such things to the grandparents? The answer is that some parents do for a variety of valid and less than valid reasons!

Ending Up in Court

If the issue can't be resolved by out-of-court negotiations, it's off they go to court. The first step is for the grandparents to request visitation rights. Such a request can be made in the form of a simple letter to the court.

The judge may then order that the grandparents and the parents or guardians attempt to mediate a resolution. The location of this mediation will be in the county where the children reside. The grandparents must pay all the costs.

Should the mediation fail, the grandparents can take the next step and become part of the divorce proceedings (just for matters of visitation). A lawyer can provide advice on how to sign on to the divorce.

In addition to the testimony of the parties at the trial, the court may require that a home study investigation be conducted. This involves the judge appointing an investigator who consults with everyone having information regarding the child and the expected custodial arrangements. A report is prepared and submitted to the court. The cost of this study is also the responsibility of the grandparents.

Taking things up a notch, a guardian *ad litem* (defined in the custody chapter) may be appointed. The guardian *ad litem* will represent the children in the legal proceedings. He or she may sometimes conduct the home study investigation as well. The judge determines which party (or parties) pays the cost of the guardian *ad litem*.

Depending on the age of the youngsters, the judge may also question them regarding their own wishes.

Finally, after hearing all the testimony, etc., the judge reaches a decision that becomes part of the final divorce judgment.

So if things go the trial route, it's very possible that four or even five lawyers will be involved! One for the grandparents (two if both sets are looking for rights) and one for each of the parents plus the guardian *ad litem*. Is this really how everyone wants to spend their money?

Besides, the divorce trial isn't the only opportunity grandparents have. At the time of the divorce the grandparents can try relying on the permission of the parents to see the kids. If later on the parents withdraw this permission, the grandparents can then file a motion with the court that seeks to gain visitation rights by modifying the final judgment.

Going All the Way

Sometimes grandparents want complete control over the children. They seek to gain primary physical and legal custody or even to be appointed as guardians. Adoption may be their goal. You can imagine that these results occur only under extreme circumstances.

Such a circumstance would be if the parent with primary physical custody is, or becomes, unfit to take care of the children (drug addiction, abusive, etc.). Other reasons would be if that parent dies or can no longer perform the parental functions (severe physical disability, mental instability, etc.).

In these situations primary physical custody as well as legal custody generally go to the other parent. However, the judge may feel that living with the other parent is not in the best interest of the children. Maybe the other parent has the same vices as the primary physical custody parent, or perhaps he or she doesn't want physical custody.

Of course it isn't enough for the judge to rule that the parents are not suitable. The court must then determine that staying with the grandparents is in the best interest of the kids and that they are able to provide an adequate and stable environment. Generally, Missouri courts give preference to relatives in such situations. This preference remains even if the parent related to the grandparent dies.

Physical or legal custody will never be granted simply because the grandparents feel that the parents don't have enough money to adequately provide for the kids. Missouri offers a full range of welfare, healthcare, and child-care programs. If a parent is willing to make a reasonable effort, no judge will completely take away custody.

Guardianship and Adoption

Unlike custody, which may be shared with others, a guardian has 100% control and authority over a child 24 hours a day. That means complete responsibility to provide for the youngster's education, medical care, support, etc.

Guardianship may be granted by the court under the following situations:

1. The child has no living parent.

2. The parents are unwilling, unfit, or unable to act as a guardian.

3. The parental rights of the parents have been terminated by the court.

Guardianships represent a temporary status. It can be removed later on if the situation with the parents improves. In any event it automatically terminates when the child reaches 18 years of age.

In rare cases where neither parent wants custody of the children (abandonment), the grandparents can seek to adopt the children. This is done almost always with the consent of the parents. Unlike a guardianship, adoption is permanent.

Going for guardianship or adoption is an entirely different process from simply seeking visitation rights. Guardianship is decided by the Probate Court and adoption by the Juvenile Court.

If the grandparents feel the parents are unfit, they can seek the support of Missouri's Children's Division. This state department has the responsibility to protect children who are abused, neglected, etc.

The Chances of Winning

Frankly, it's rare for a Missouri court to overrule parental preference regarding a grandparent's visitation rights. It's even less likely that grandparents will obtain guardianship of the children.

However, if the situation has merit, it wouldn't be the first time that the court granted such requests.

The best solution for grandparents is to be nice to their daughter and son-in-law or son and daughter-in-law before the divorce so they will be welcomed after the divorce.

CHAPTER 10

Maintenance

The Painful Truth

"**M**OST PEOPLE CAN'T AFFORD to get divorced." That statement was made by a judge. A judge should know.

Nevertheless, more than 40,000 Missourians divorce each year. Many caught up in the process cling to the hope that alimony from their former spouses will help keep the wheels turning. Those on the "likely to pay" side of the equation, meanwhile, believe that after the split, it should be everyone for themselves. Well, times have changed even if peoples' hopes and dreams haven't.

To begin with, in Missouri it's not called alimony any longer. Courts now refer to such payments as "maintenance." You may also hear it called "spousal support" or just plain "support."

Number two: No one in Missouri is automatically entitled to or excluded from spousal support. In fact, Missouri's Supreme Court hasn't set any guidelines. So it's left up to the judge's discretion when determining whether maintenance will be awarded, along with how much and for how long. Those decisions just can't be predicted with any certainty.

What's certain is that if maintenance isn't ordered in the final divorce judgment, neither party can request it in the future regardless of what significant changes have taken place.

None of this means that courts operate on the level of the Wild West. Indeed, there are quite a few established factors that the court will consider as it goes about deciding on spousal support. That being said, it's still risky business.

Reaching the First Plateau

Anyway, let's test the likelihood of your receiving maintenance by answering the following two questions.

1. *Do you lack sufficient property, including marital property received as part of the divorce, to provide for your needs?*

This first question is asking whether you earn enough income from your property to pay your bills. It is not talking about selling your property. The judge cannot make you support yourself by using up the property awarded to you.

2. *Are you unable to support your needs through a job, or are you the custodian of a child whose condition or circumstances make it inappropriate for you to work?*

Don't forget, the court assumes just about everyone is employable, but there are special circumstances where it's either not enough or not feasible.

This is strictly a pass-or-fail examination. If you can't convince the court that the answer to both questions is yes, then the maintenance money train is leaving the station and you're not on board. But, of course, your former better half may have a reserved seat.

Now for the Hard Part

So we have a reason to continue with the rest of this chapter, let's assume that you or your spouse passes the preceding two-question test. Remember, the only issue clarified so far is that one party needs maintenance. Determining whether the final judgment will actually include support is often a more complicated affair.

Before any money changes hands, the judge will want to know what the other side can afford to pay and how long the need for this financial assistance will go on.

Ten questions are used to figure all this out.

1. *What are the financial resources of the person asking for maintenance?*

You may think this question was already addressed when the requesting spouse reached the first plateau. In general that is true.

But, in the earlier two question test the judge only determined that the requesting spouse's resources were inadequate. That is the starting point for the analysis. The court must now take those resources into account when determining how much money the receiving spouse is going to get.

2. *How much time is needed to retrain the person seeking maintenance?*

Often one spouse has been working at a low paying part-time job or perhaps not at all. That was all right when the other side delivered a paycheck every week, but now things will certainly be different.

One way of keeping maintenance payments down is to give the low paid spouse time to learn a marketable job skill. This might require only a few months (perhaps getting a real estate license) or several years (getting an accounting degree). Letting the judge in on your career training plans is a good idea.

3. What is the relative earning power of each person?

If you and your soon to be ex-spouse both make the same amount of money (disregarding any child responsibilities for the moment), it isn't likely that maintenance payments are in the future for either side.

Of course, if one party makes a lot more than the other, the judge may be willing to share that good fortune. But the other spouse must still demonstrate a need. Support isn't usually focused on sharing the wealth equally. And it isn't meant to be a punishment.

4. What was the standard of living during the marriage?

In divorce many things are dealt with on a relative basis. In this regard, you can be assured that the court will deal with Donald Trump's divorce differently from how it will your own. This theory of relativity plays an important part in deciding how much, if any, maintenance gets ordered.

Mr. Trump and his wife (choose one) had a certain lifestyle during their marriage, and so did you, though yours may have been a bit different from "The Donald's." The judge will use this specific living standard as a guide when figuring out whether a spouse's request is reasonable.

So just what is a "standard of living"? Well, it has to do with the kind of house a couple had, the cars they drove, how often they went on vacation and out to dinner, the clothes they wore, etc.

If one side has enough resources to keep both parties at the level they enjoyed during their marriage, a judge may try to do just that. But more often it's a starting point for determining how much both parties will lose.

The reality is that after most divorces the standard of living for everyone declines. Five-bedroom colonials become three-bedroom ranches. Three-bedroom ranches get reduced to two-bedroom apartments. The judge will try to spread the pain on a more or less equal basis.

   5. *What are the debts and assets each person got from the divorce?*

Deciding on spousal support isn't only about income. Property counts too when calculating how each side comes out of a divorce. Someone with a low income but a lot of assets can invest some of them (the court generally won't order people to sell assets for this purpose) to either reduce or eliminate the need for support. Looking at it the other way, a spouse with a lot of assets but limited earned income may still be able to provide substantial maintenance payments.

But don't ignore that great asset killer called debt. If one party gets saddled with property burdened with loans and mortgages, it can be hard, if not impossible, for him or her to come up with support payments.

Judges reluctant to award maintenance may simply give some extra assets to the needy party and leave it at that. So keep this discussion in mind later on when you're reading the property chapter about dividing up the Porsche Boxster, the silver service for 24, and that Mad River canoe.

   6. *How long was the marriage?*

Not how long did if feel like, but how long was it actually in terms of days and weeks. Some states put a lot of emphasis on marriage length, but in Missouri it's just another consideration.

For example, a Kirksville couple was married in November, but the holidays proved challenging, and the New Year's celebration wasn't a happy one. By the time Valentine's Day rolled around the divorce was under way.

Even a Missouri court will view that couple differently from one in Dunklin who were married 22 years before splitting up. The longer the marriage, the more commingled are the assets and the earning power. Also, the greater the obligation each spouse has to the other.

   7. *What is the age and physical and emotional condition of each person?*

Think of age and health issues as the spice that flavors the other nine questions discussed in this section. The court looks at a spouse who is 25 years old differently from one coming up on 65. But put that younger spouse in a head-on collision resulting in total paralysis and now health and not age is the most important factor. The same goes for a partner having serious mental or emotional problems.

Normally, a judge dealing with a two-year marriage is inclined to give no support. But, introduce a permanently disabled spouse, and the other side could be looking at a lifetime obligation.

   8. *What does the person who would pay the support need to survive?*

Who says that the Missouri court doesn't have a heart? A judge will have no desire to see the paying spouse driving around in a 1958 Edsel Ranger while the receiving side romps down the road in a bright red Audi convertible.

As mentioned earlier, maintenance isn't used to punish one side or reward the other. There has to be a reasonable balance when all things are considered.

9. How did each party act during the marriage?

OK, maybe maintenance isn't exactly about revenge, but poor performers might still be held accountable. So if the potentially paying spouse was a drunk or an abuser or did not fully live up to the wedding vows on a regular basis, a judge could lean toward being more generous with the support amount than otherwise would be the case.

However, following the divorce there is frequently little excess cash available to teach anyone a lesson. Don't get your hopes up.

10. Are there any other relevant issues?

Every marriage contains a unique set of circumstances. It's important to bring these special factors to the judge's attention.

It's Like Making Sausage

Clearly, a judge must consider a lot of factors before deciding on spousal support. The final decision is one of the most difficult items to predict. While no official guidelines exist, there are some fundamental concepts to keep in mind that can provide the parties an idea of how things will go.

The first is that if the court decides that maintenance is appropriate, the likelihood is that the order will extend "indefinitely." Indefinitely doesn't mean forever. It means until one of five things occurs: the paying spouse dies, the receiving spouse dies, the receiving spouse remarries, the maintenance is no longer needed, or the paying party can no longer afford to pay it.

Second, Missouri law doesn't provide for "rehabilitative maintenance" (payments just long enough to allow the receiving party to get on his or her feet after the divorce). If there is a short-term foreseeable change (graduating from law school in 18 months or a child starting school in a year so the custodial parent can return to a career), support may be limited to just that necessary period, but it's rarely done.

And third, marriage length does have an influence on obligations. The court is more inclined to consider maintenance the longer the marriage lasted. This is particularly true if the receiving spouse is nearing retirement.

These three general rules will hopefully keep you grounded on the positive side of reality.

God Bless the Children

So far this chapter has ignored the elephant in the corner of the room—the children. Kids can dramatically change the situation. The court is more concerned with maintaining the children's living standard than it is about keeping an equal standard of living between the two spouses.

Maintenance shouldn't be confused with child support. If the court is trying to maintain the children's living standard, that money will be awarded through child support. However, judges will give consideration to the entire amount of support—maintenance and child support—to try to take care of the children's needs.

This doesn't mean that the kids' living standard won't decline if funds are limited. The court recognizes that in most cases the children will be spending time at the home of the parent paying support as well. Money has to be available to make this second home at least safe, presentable, and able to accommodate overnights with the kids. Nevertheless, preference will be given to the home where the children are primarily based.

The story gets more complicated if the paying parent has the children for a large percentage of the time or there was an award of split physical custody (see the custody chapter for definitions). In these cases the judge may try to balance the incomes more equally.

Divorce has a lot of interconnected parts. Read this chapter along with those on child custody, child support, and property distribution to get the total picture of what to expect. After all, it's a zero-sum game. The greater the child support payment, the less money available for maintenance.

Adjusting Spousal Support

When judges order maintenance, it is almost always open ended and modifiable (the final judgment must state that it can be modified in order to be adjusted in the future). When situations change, the paying or receiving party will have to seek a modification. While child support is the easiest item to get modified, given good reasons, adjusting a maintenance payment isn't far behind in simplicity. Once spousal support is written into the final order, it can be extended indefinitely or cut short. The amount may be made to go up or down.

For example, a Mound City woman who had been paying support to an invalid ex-husband was able to get the maintenance payments reduced after he inherited a large amount of money. In another case an ex-wife in Florissant received an increase in support when a medical problem prevented her from continuing to work.

Generally, spousal support payments (not child support) will automatically end if the receiving party remarries. But the same is not automatically true if the former spouse is just living with someone. Judges never write specific cohabitation (living together) provisions into maintenance orders. Still, a reduction was possible for a Camdenton man whose ex-wife took on a live-in boyfriend. He proved to the court that her new honey was paying a significant share of his ex-wife's expenses.

The flip side of this situation isn't the same. If the paying party gets a lover, friend or relative to move in and share expenses, the court won't hear arguments that he or she can now afford to pay more.

Also, the law requires the receiving party to make a continuing good-faith effort to become self-supporting. It's possible for the paying spouse to get relief from spousal support if it can be shown that the other party is out playing golf every day rather than pursuing employment.

Finally, spousal support normally doesn't include a cost-of-living adjustment. Over time it may be necessary to return to court and get an inflationary increase.

A Good Thing about Maintenance

Maintenance is tax deductible for the payer, so at least it gets paid using pretax dollars. On the other hand, the receiving party must pay income tax on any support payment. With some planning this can work to everyone's advantage.

Take a couple from East Prairie. John is a businessman in the 30% tax bracket. Elaine, his soon to be ex-spouse, is just getting back into the job market and resides in the 15% column.

John pays Elaine $1,000 a month in maintenance. Because this payment is tax deductible, the payment costs him only $700 (he saves $300 in taxes). Meanwhile, Elaine is paying only 15% tax on the $1,000, which amounts to $150. This is a net tax savings of $150 a month ($300 minus $150).

Smart couples will take advantage of such tax-saving opportunities by structuring the child support and maintenance payments in a manner that maximizes the total number of dollars available to both parties and the children.

Putting Your Spouse under Contract

But the court has no interest in competing with H&R Block. If the parties want to implement such a tax strategy, they had better work it out on their own, using something called "contractual maintenance."

With contractual maintenance, the parties, not the judge, decide on a specific plan for spousal support. It can be tied to the asset transfer or other aspects of the divorce so both sides feel that, in total, it's a fair deal.

Because the parties do the negotiation, contractual maintenance is as flexible as they want to make it. Payments can reflect the changing needs of the family—perhaps more money when the kids are growing up and less after they move out or when the parties retire.

Another benefit of contractual maintenance is that there can be a clear end point. If the court imposes spousal support, there is often no certainty as to when it will end. Usually, the final judgment will not indicate a final payment date.

With contractual maintenance the final payment date is
normally specified. Unless it is specifically allowed under
the agreement, it's not subject to alteration by the court.

The receiving party also benefits. If things get left up to
the judge, there's a risk that no support will be provided.
Should it be granted and then the receiving party has a
favorable change in circumstances, the paying side can
go back to court and get the maintenance reduced or
even stopped. This normally isn't the case with contractual maintenance. The terms of the contract can't be
modified up or down. Also, depending on what the parties agree to, the payments may continue should the
receiving side remarry (although this is unusual).

Finally, the paying spouse is often willing to make higher payments in exchange for getting a specific ending
date and avoiding the possibility of payment increases.

The Story of Jim and Josie

Sometimes there are important unknowns down the
road. This was the case for Jim from Flat River. Jim
injured his brain stem in a bicycle accident during the
marriage. He was able to continue working, but the
court was convinced that the injury might become a
problem in the future.

So while the judge made no order of maintenance in the
final judgment, she did indicate in the judgment that the
issue was open and modifiable. Some judges might go
further and order the uninjured side to pay a nominal
maintenance of one dollar a year (also indicated to be
modifiable).

By doing either of these two things the court keeps the
door open for Jim to receive substantial spousal support
payments later on should his injury take a turn for the

worse. Remember, if the judge doesn't specifically state that the decision not to give maintenance is modifiable (as was done in Jim's case) or actually orders modifiable maintenance (as little as a dollar), maintenance can never be added or modified in the future.

And once that door is closed on maintenance, it's closed forever. So if the kids are young or the health of a party is in question, it can certainly pay dividends if the potentially receiving side is able to persuade the judge to include the possibility of future spousal support. Often this isn't easy to do.

A Disappointing Chapter

Ending the chapter this way is disappointing. Many readers will be still uncertain if spousal support is in their future (paying or receiving). Unfortunately, even lawyers have trouble predicting this event.

Everyone needs to have realistic expectations of what a judge is likely to provide to each side. Better yet, if some level of support is reasonably required, the parties should work out a deal between themselves (contractual maintenance) and avoid rolling the dice in court.

CHAPTER 11

Property Distribution

The Starting Point Is Always the Same

JUDGES BEGIN every divorce proceeding with the assumption that all property possessed by the couple should be equally divided. This doesn't mean that's how it will eventually turn out. As explained below, there are a number of factors that determine who is entitled to what.

It does mean that in order for the judge to alter this initial position, one of the parties has to provide convincing evidence that a 50–50 split isn't in keeping with the law or simply isn't fair and balanced.

What Are Property and Assets

The terms "property" and "assets" are used interchangeably in this book. Both stand for anything having monetary value. This includes cash, stocks, bonds, real estate, automobiles, homes, furniture, jewelry, cows, horses, pension plans, antiques, an Ozzie Smith autographed baseball card, etc.

168

Property/assets are different from income. Income is an anticipated future cash flow. Property/assets are what remain of income that was received in the past.

Missouri's Equitable Distribution

Most states utilize some variety of what is referred to as "equitable distribution" when dividing up the couple's assets. Under the equitable distribution concept the court is given a degree of discretion, based on the facts of the case, when dividing the assets in its final order. Depending on the state, such laws can allow a lot or a little wiggle room for the judge.

Some equitable distribution states don't differentiate between property acquired before and during the marriage. They put all the spouses' assets into one pile, and the court hands them out in whatever way the judge thinks is fair. While Missouri wants to be equitable, that's a bit too radical.

So, like many equitable distribution states, Missouri separates assets into "marital property" (everything acquired during the marriage, with a few exceptions) and "separate property" (everything acquired prior to the marriage, also with some possible alterations).

A Missouri court always gives 100% of the separate assets to the spouse who brought them to the marriage. But when it comes to the marital assets, Show-Me State judges can shuffle that deck any way they feel is fair. That being said, the court must be given a good reason not to split the marital property 50–50.

While it may be comforting to learn that Missouri's goal is to be fair, that isn't necessarily everyone's personal objective. If you're the less needy spouse, it's possible that you'll get less than half the marriage assets.

Separate vs. Marital Property

This isn't the time to be "loosey goosey" about under-standing the difference between separate and marital property. Getting it right is tremendously important, and it's not as easy as it sounds. So let's go through a few examples to sharpen your legal skills.

Missouri divorce law has the following five specific ways of identifying separate property. Everything out-side of these definitions is marital property and can be given to either party in whatever proportion the judge feels is equitable.

> 1. *Property acquired by gift, devise, bequest or descent;*

Any gift given to only one of the spouses is a separate asset, even if received during the marriage. That includes the anniversary gifts one spouse gives the other and the inheritance from Aunt Frieda given in your name only. The motive for giving the gift doesn't matter to the judge.

And separate ownership is immediate. So don't go looking to get back that 24-carat gold wedding ring if the marriage falls apart the first weekend following the honeymoon.

> 2. *Property acquired in exchange for property acquired prior to the marriage or in exchange for property acquired by gift bequest, devise, or descent;*

Follow the money. Say that one spouse brings a Cessna Skylane aircraft (the best all-round light aircraft ever!) into the marriage. Eventually it gets sold, with the pro-ceeds going to purchase a summer home on a lake near Laurie. Is the house separate or marital property?

It's not enough to say, "My wife and I agreed that the lake home would be mine alone." The judge is going to want all the information on the sale of the plane and pur-chase of the house. Was the Cessna fully paid for when it came into the marriage? Whose name is on the deed and the mortgage of the house? Where did the funds come from to pay the mortgage? Were any marital funds used in the purchase? What did each spouse do with respect to repairing and upgrading the house? Get the picture?

For a long time the name on the asset's title or deed meant everything when the court was classifying property. Today, where the money came from to make the acquisition is almost as important. And just because separate funds are commingled with marital funds doesn't automatically make the resulting purchase entirely a marital asset. It's possible for the judge to decide that 40% of something is marital property and 60% is a separate asset based on the source of funds.

Unless there is evidence to the contrary, the court is going to look at property as follows:

- An asset purchased with marital funds is marital property even if it is separately titled.

- An asset purchased with separate funds is marital property if it is jointly titled (the assumption is that the noncontributing party's share was a gift from the other spouse).

To avoid any legal misunderstandings, record keeping is essential, and that's usually the problem 20 years after the sale and purchase. "He said/she said" testimony will not win the day. Fail to show a strong paper trail, and expect to be splitting the property with your ex-spouse.

  3. *Property acqured by a spouse after a decree of legal separation;*

A legal separation allows for the division of property just

as it's done in a divorce. If the legally separated couple decides to divorce, any property acquired after the separation is treated as separate property. It belongs only to the spouse who acquired it.

4. *Property excluded by valid written agreement;*

We are talking now about prenuptial (before the marriage) and postnuptial (during the marriage) agreements. These documents actually work. If the parties agreed in advance who will own what property following a divorce, the court is happy to enforce that arrangement. While the judge will not consider whether the result is what a court would have done, if it is grossly unfair, it might still be overturned.

That being said, if there's a lot of money at stake, it's likely that the side less well off will challenge the pre- or postnuptial agreement. So it's important that a lawyer for each of the parties reviews such an agreement before it's signed to ensure it will be upheld. Of course, it's a little too late to be talking about that now. Hopefully, yours was done the right way.

Please note: When one spouse signs a waiver of marital interest on an asset purchased by the other spouse with marital funds, the property remains a marital asset. These waivers are usually executed to facilitate a business deal or to allow one of the spouses to buy a house at separation but before the divorce is final. If you haven't signed one, then there's no need to worry about this fine point.

5. *The increase in value of property acquired prior to the marriage or pursuant to subdivisions 1 to 4 of 452.330.2 RSMo, unless marital assets including labor have contributed to such increases and then only to the extent of such contributions.*

Did you get all that? The following example will help clarify things, but first note that this kind of issue is likely to put a lot of money into your lawyer's pocket.

Here goes: A woman gets married owning a business worth $150,000. After the wedding, the business continues to grow in value. By the time she is getting divorced, it's worth $350,000. The judge wants to know why.

If it grew because it was managed well by the spouse who owned it or due to inflation, etc., the entire value is separate property. But if it grew because the nonowner spouse was active in the business and made a meaningful contribution, or if the owner spouse didn't take any income in order to inflate the retained earnings, then some or all of the $200,000 growth ($350,000 minus $150,000) that took place during the marriage is likely to be considered a marital asset. This is often a tough sell, however. The fact that the nonowner merely hosted business dinners and accompanied the owner on business trips won't cut it.

Keep in mind we are considering only the increase in what the business is worth. The income from the business paid to the owners during the marriage is always a marital asset.

Just answering question five isn't enough. You have to prove it. Many expensive arguments can be made in court pro and con. Often detailed records are not available. That doesn't mean it's not worth the effort. But be rational and avoid the deep end of the pool. If the gain isn't worth the expense (considering the likelihood of winning and the values involved), try to work things out with your spouse.

Remember, the court starts with the assumption that all assets are marital property. It's up to one of the parties to prove which ones are separate property.

A Plethora of Potpourri

A little bit of legal knowledge is often dangerous. The following information is provided mainly to demonstrate how complicated determining marital and separate property can be. The real lesson being taught is that if the amount in question is significant, it's best to seek professional advice.

Stocks or savings accounts brought into the marriage and kept in just one spouse's name are normally nonmarital assets. Here's the tricky part. While any *appreciation* (did the stock go up in value?) experienced on these items during the marriage is also separate property, the *interest and dividends* received from these investments during the union are marital property. That's because interest and dividends are considered income, and all income earned during the marriage is a marital asset.

If one spouse has a preliminary interest in an asset before the marriage (lawyers refer to this as an "inchoate interest"), but it's not finalized until after the marriage, that goes in the books as separate property. On the other hand, such an asset would be marital property if the interest was created during the marriage but payment was to come after the divorce.

One example of this is a tax refund earned prior to the marriage but received afterward. That's a separate asset. Another example is a claim for lost wages made during the marriage but settled and payment received after the divorce. That money is definitely marital property.

When an asset, such as a house, is purchased before the marriage, but paid for, at least in part, during the marriage (such as by paying off a mortgage), the property may be separate but have a partial marital interest.

If a spouse is getting disability payments, the value of the payments received during the marriage is marital property, while the payments due him or her after the divorce are considered separate property. When the disability payment is paid in a lump sum during the marriage, the amount meant as compensation for lost earnings for the period after the divorce is also a nonmarital asset.

A future stream of royalties, insurance renewals, commissions, etc., reflecting compensation for work that took place during the marriage is marital property.

To summarize: Income earned during the marriage, either through a job or an investment (even an investment of separate property) is marital property. However, if a separate property investment appreciates in value (again, this growth doesn't include income it produces from earnings, interest, dividends, rents, etc.), that asset and its growth value are nonmarital property.

Splitting Up the Marital Assets

Ask any good Missouri divorce attorney the basis for deciding the marital property distribution and instantly he or she will rattle off the following five key elements that all judges must factor into their final decisions.

> 1. *The economic circumstances of each spouse at the time the division of property is to become effective, including the desirability of awarding the family home or the right to live therein for reasonable periods to the spouse having custody of any children*

What chance does each spouse have to move up the corporate ladder? One or both might never even find the ladder.

Maybe one party has unusually high medical expenses. Is he or she able to work at all? Is one supporting an elderly parent, etc? The court will consider these special circumstances. The judge will also be thinking about the assets necessary for retirement.

This element specifically mentions awarding the family home. But it doesn't separate the family home from the rest of the assets when considering what is a fair division. If the primary custodial parent gets the house, its value is factored into the judge's decision regarding how the remaining property is divided.

Also, just because a spouse gets the family home doesn't mean that all the equity (home value minus the mortgage) goes to that spouse. The equity is often split between the parties. (See the chapter on property issues and considerations.)

2. *The contribution of each spouse to the acquisition of the marital property, including the contribution of a spouse as homemaker*

Did both sides contribute equally to create the marital property? "Equally" doesn't necessarily refer to an equal contribution of income.

Many working spouses assume that since they were the ones bringing home the bacon, their role in acquiring property was more important than that of the other party who stayed home with the kids, cooking the bacon. Missouri law, however, explicitly requires a court to consider the stay-at-home's contributions as well.

In such cases, the efforts of the supporting spouse helped create the hefty income stream even if the other party is earning the money. The stay-at-home spouse will be rewarded with a fair share of the assets (and maybe even some spousal support).

3. *The value of the nonmarital property set apart to each spouse*

You may think that this one doesn't sound fair. What's the point of having a separate asset category if the court tries to even things out when dividing up the marital property? You're right, and in most cases a judge is reluctant to put too much weight on this element. And certainly the court will not compensate the poor spouse on a dollar-for-dollar basis.

But, if one spouse has ample assets and general prosperity while the other is suffering a financial heart attack, the judge may try to help out the poorer spouse. Under these conditions it pays for the rich spouse to make a compassionate impression with court.

4. *The conduct of the parties during the marriage*

Did one party commit adultery or abuse the other? Was either spouse drunk all the time or did he or she fail to work steadily inside or outside of the home due to a lack of effort? Is it payback time? Maybe, but probably not.

5. *Custodial arrangements for minor children*

The court is concerned about maintaining the standard of living and general normalcy for the minor children. If money is tight for the parent gaining primary physical custody, the judge may award a greater percentage of the assets to that parent in order to help out the kids. Yes, this can also be addressed with support payments, but sometimes that's not enough.

What It All Means

Anyone reading the preceding section jumps on the factors that are in his or her favor. "I did all the work. If it weren't for me, there would be nothing to split up." Or, "That bum has been cheating on me since the honeymoon." Or, "I stayed at home raising the kids; how can I start earning a living at my age?" And so on and so on.

The first thing to realize is that not all the five elements have the same importance. Spouses who put up with lying, cheating, and drunkenness for 20 years are surprised to find that the conduct of the parties is often at the bottom of the totem pole in Missouri (see the section "Bad, Bad Leroy Brown").

Regardless of how rich or poor the parties are, the court maintains the same priorities. Children come first, spousal support payments, if required, are second, and the rest is third.

However, there still needs to be a balance in the final order. A judge isn't going to give everything to the kids and a needy spouse so they can maintain a high living standard while the other spouse is left to starve.

When money is tight, everyone is expected to sacrifice, and this is very often the case. Few people gain financially through divorce. Frequently, both sides lose a lot of ground as they discover it was much cheaper living together.

The Long and Short of It

Sometimes, whether the marriage was long or short can have an effect on the division of assets. But Missouri doesn't define a long marriage as clearly as do some states.

For example in Vermont a long marriage is generally one of 15 years or greater. In other states, such as California, it can be a union lasting only 10 years. These courts view a couple with a long marriage as having a complete partnership that includes long-term obligations to each other's well-being. This total obligation gets expressed in the divorce judgment by how the maintenance (alimony) and assets are assigned.

Missouri doesn't define what a long marriage is either by legal statute or by tradition. But judges certainly do view the obligations of the parties to each other in a two-year union differently than if it were one of 20 years. The longer the marriage, the stronger the claim the poorer spouse will have on marital assets (even in excess of 50%), though the greatest impact of a long marriage is usually on maintenance.

Bad, Bad Leroy Brown

Many people believe that adultery has a big influence on the judge's decision, but it rarely does. This is especially true if it occurs after the separation. Other considerations are simply more important. The moral character of the partners is usually not much of an issue in reaching the final judgment.

All this is not to say that a spouse's poor conduct is always ignored. Physical abuse or behavior that created a great mental burden on the innocent spouse can be an influencing factor. An affair that consumed enough money to impact the marital finances might get some attention from the court as well. It's up to the judge, but a 5% to 10% penalty is only likely in a severe case.

Bad behavior can also make the judge feel that the person isn't trustworthy, resulting in the final order requiring him or her to pay more things immediately and to have less control over future issues.

Remember, punishing a spouse isn't the judge's main
objective. Your wishes may differ substantially from the
court's on this point.

A Football Draft

Splitting up household goods can be tough. Most people's houses (those of the authors included) are full of
used furniture that just isn't worth nearly what it cost
new, even if it was bought last month. And consider the
cost of lawyers dividing up your goodies at a combined
hourly rate of $500 or more. Or the judge trying to value
a set of Precious Moments figurines versus a Snap-On
tool set. It's a challenge to reach a satisfactory outcome.

Many couples decide to avoid having the court tell them
who gets what and do it themselves. One favored way
of going about it is similar to the football draft.

Step 1—Walk through the house and make a list of everything.

Step 2—Each spouse independently puts his or her list in
order, making the item a party wants most number 1 and
the item that party wants least at the bottom of the list.

Step 3—Flip a coin to see who goes first.

Step 4—The first party gets to choose the first item he or
she wants and it goes back and forth from then on.

An item that is disproportionately expensive may have
to be dealt with differently. For example, if one side
wants the Picasso, that party may have to give up a number of early-rounds picks on the rest of the household
goods so things remain in balance.

Using this method both sides get most of what they want
and save the legal fees.

A Sentimental Journey

Marital property that has both monetary and sentimental value is always part of the total asset inventory. So, if you want your favorite antique hooked carpet, expect to get less of something else.

Telling the judge of your special attachment is no guarantee you'll be seeing it under your name in the final judgment. If both spouses are fighting over something, the court may simply order it sold and the money split. Judges just don't have time to spare. So much for sentiment.

Items that have only sentimental value get even less attention by the court. So if the parties don't want to see a for sale sign stapled to Maple the cat, they had better find a better solution between themselves.

Please, it's definitely going to be a long divorce if the couple can't even agree about things having little economic value. Everyone really has to try harder!

CHAPTER 12

Property Issues and Considerations

Matters of Life and Debt

BANKS, CREDIT CARD COMPANIES, and automobile manufacturers own a good portion of what people call their property. We are reminded of this each month as the payments come due. So it's important to consider this debt when valuing assets.

Obviously, a $400,000 farm with a $350,000 mortgage has a value of $50,000 for the divorcing couple. Less obvious is the fact that having debt on an asset automatically reduces its value beyond the money that's owed.

Consider the situation of a couple in Vandalia getting divorced. The combined value of their assets is $250,000. However, they also have debts totaling $100,000. So their property represents only $150,000 in equity ($250,000 less $100,000).

The divorce settlement grants each side half of the equity ($75,000 each). However, one party receives assets worth $75,000 having no debt, while the other gets property valued at $175,000 but having $100,000 of debt. Which one is better off?

Most people would rather have the assets with no debt attached. Forget, for the moment, any sentimental or practical value certain assets have even if there is debt on them. After the divorce, monthly payments that used to be hard to make may become impossible to make.

In the end, a spouse often finds it necessary to sell the debt-ridden property and pay off the loan. In the case of real estate the selling costs can be substantial (and if there's pressure to sell, the results may be less than optimal). If a hunting camp is worth $45,000 and the debt on it is $15,000, its value in the property division is $30,000. However, if it has to be sold after the divorce because there's not enough money for the monthly payments it will cost about $1,800 in fees for the selling broker.

The court rarely takes this $1,800 commission cost into account when doing the asset split unless the sale is anticipated at the time of the divorce. So if you plan on having to dispose of a major asset, make sure the judge knows about it. Otherwise, you'll be paying that sales commission all by yourself later on.

Dividing Up Debt

The court must divide debt in the same manner it divides property. Often this means assigning the debt to the party who received the benefit (the asset or the entertainment value). So if you get the car, you will normally get the car loan. If a credit card paid for a vacation, you may be able to convince a judge to make the one who got the suntan pay for that card. If both parties enjoyed the sun, this will have to be allocated to one party at the time of the divorce as part of the total asset and debt split.

The judge also looks at what debt was accumulated after the separation and will generally distribute it to the party who created it. A common exception is when one side generates debt in order to pay for food, housing, schooling the children, etc., because the other party failed to provide a fair amount of support. In this case the court will be looking at all of the financial circumstances to decide how to allocate the debt.

Finally, consideration is given to each spouse's overall ability to take on the debt burden. It usually makes no sense to bankrupt one party when the other has sufficient funds to handle more than his or her share of what is owed.

It's Hard to Escape Debt

If the two parties were legally responsible for a debt before the divorce, then both remain legally responsible for it after the marriage from the point of view of the lender.

While the court can designate who must pay the debt, there is no way it can remove a spouse's name from a loan obligation. If the spouse assigned the debt by the court fails to make the payments, the lender can legally go after the other party.

Sure, the innocent party may sue the designated ex-spouse for failure to pay. But this takes time and money. And what if the designated party is broke or dies and the estate has no funds to pay off the debt? The innocent party will probably have to make good on all remaining payments.

For example, suppose both spouses sign a loan to buy a 2008 Hummer. (Who saw that gas crisis coming?) In the divorce settlement the husband gets the Hummer and responsibility for the debt. Unfortunately, the payments stop six months later when he's killed while totaling the car.

If the car was uninsured (another payment he forgot to make), the auto loan company will go after both the former husband's estate and the other spouse to collect the debt. The same would be true if the husband defaults on the loan because he loses his job. It's not the loan company's fault the couple got divorced.

Big money gets involved when the debt in question is a $125,000 mortgage signed by both spouses on the marital home. The judge will sometimes try to reduce this risk by ordering the party getting the house to make a good-faith effort to refinance it under his or her name only. This can be easier said than done.

Indeed, while it's smart to have all debt refinanced under the name of the responsible person following the divorce, most judges won't make this kind of order. Anyway, just as in the case of the marital home, lenders are often unwilling to write a new loan based on the income of just one spouse.

Admit the Ship Is Sinking

Sometimes you simply can't get from here to there. The cost of child support, spousal support, and paying for two households with an income that barely supported one before the divorce can be overwhelming. Parents need to provide a proper house and living standard for their kids. Even without children the debt payments can be too much. The only choice may be bankruptcy.

Under bankruptcy law (with some limitations) the parties can keep the homes in which they live, along with their cars, furniture, clothes, and a small amount of money. While their other assets will be lost, they would have lost them anyway since there was no way to keep up the payments.

A Note About Home Equity

When the judge looks over the marital property, the first item to get split 50–50 is often the equity in the marital home (the difference between what the house is worth today and the mortgage). Even if there are other sizable assets the judge may still want the home equity shared. An exception might be when the amount of other assets (retirement funds, investments, etc.) is so substantial that they can easily balance things out.

The process for determining the equity amount may be a little surprising. Rather than valuing the house, the judge sometimes takes the simpler route of ordering the house sold, with the equity split as directed in the final order.

If the judge does award the marital home to the spouse having primary custody, most often this spouse must pay the other party at the time of the divorce a specific sum of money representing the houseless spouse's share of the home's equity. If this isn't possible, the equity payment may be delayed until the house is sold or refinanced. The payment is rarely postponed past the day the children are no longer entitled to be supported.

The payment going to the party without the house could include an interest component to compensate for the delay (the time between the divorce and the payment date), but not always. However, if there is a specific amount to be paid (rather than simply a share of the equity based on whatever the house eventually sells for), it will carry "post-judgment interest" at the rate of 9% per year.

Traditional Pension Plans

It's understandable that many people don't think that the right to a traditional pension, the kind that pays a fixed amount each month after retiring, is property like a home or a bank account. Perhaps this pension benefit was initiated prior to the marriage and its value will continue to build well after the divorce.

No one knows what it will be worth when it's actually collected. If a person quits or is laid off before retirement age, the pension value is often greatly diminished. Perhaps the pension is not yet "vested" (usually a worker has to be with a company for a certain period of time before being guaranteed a pension payment on retirement—that's "vesting").

All that is quite true. However, a traditional pension is an asset (marital property), and it will definitely be divided when the property settlement gets hammered out. Next to the equity in the marital home, a pension may be the only other item having any substantial value. How does the court deal with it? Here are a few simple facts.

The first is that a pension is treated by the court just like any other marital property. Neither side has any special rights to it. Because of its importance with respect to retirement, the judge is likely to split the pension 50–50 rather than give it all to one party.

The second fact is that pension rights are earned over a long period of time, but it's only the specific span of time that a party was both married and earning credit toward a pension that counts in determining the distribution to the other side.

For example, if someone retired from a company after 20 years but was married for only five years during that time, then his or her spouse would be entitled to share in no more than 25% of the pension (5 years is 25% of 20 years).

A third fact is that while a pension is a promise to pay an uncertain amount of money in the future, there are ways to estimate its current value. To do this, an actuary or economist (experts in estimating such values) must be hired to testify in court.

Based on this testimony, a judge could include the pension's value with the other assets being distributed at the time of the divorce. The person earning the pension may get to keep it, but it will be balanced by other assets going to the non-pensioned spouse. However, while that certainly does happen, it's not the most common result.

One reason for this is the uncertain nature of the estimate. A second reason is that the spouse with the pension often doesn't have the money or other assets to pay the pension's value to the other side at the time of the divorce. Finally, many parties can't afford to hire a highly paid pension expert. After all that money is spent, a judge may fail to agree with the expert's proposal. In the end, the judge usually orders the pension to be shared on a monthly basis at the time it's actually collected.

To understand how this would work let's continue with the example in which the marriage represents 25% of the total pension-earning period. Assume that the working spouse retires and receives a pension amount of $1,000 a month and the sharing spouse is awarded half the pension value, a 50–50 split. This works out so the sharing spouse receives $125 a month ($125 is half of $250, which is 25% of the $1,000). The amount will be paid directly to the sharing spouse by the pension plan.

Don't Forget the QDRO

To ensure that this happens, it's critical for the pension sharing spouse, following the divorce, to immediately notify the company offering the pension (or the agent who manages the other spouse's pension fund) of the court order to split the pension. There is a chance that if the spouse earning the pension drops dead before this notification is filed, the pension-sharing spouse will get nothing.

The document used to notify the pension plan administrator is called a Qualified Domestic Relations Order (abbreviated as "QDRO" and often spoken as "quad row"). Usually, the party getting the pension share (not the party earning the pension) has an attorney prepare the QDRO. The other spouse (more likely his or her attorney) will want to review it. A certified copy (an official copy with the court clerk's seal on it) is then sent to the company offering the pension. The court is not responsible for doing this.

The QDRO informs the company of the sharing spouse's legal right to a portion of the pension. When the pension-earning party retires, the company will send the appropriate amounts directly to each side every month.

What happens to the pension if the sharing party dies before the one with the pension retires depends upon how the QDRO is written and the terms of the plan. If the QDRO has a reverter clause and the plan allows it, the spouse earning the pension can notify the court of the death, and it will rescind the QDRO. So the pension earning spouse needs to make sure a reverter clause is included in the QDRO.

If it is, the spouse who earned the pension will now get 100% of the total pension when he or she retires (less fees, if any). The estate of the dead pension-sharing spouse has no rights to the pension.

Finally, if the party who is earning the pension dies before retirement and fails to list the other party as a beneficiary of the pension, the other spouse may lose all rights to the pension. So make sure the divorce judgment and, more important, the QDRO, provides for surviving-spouse benefits.

Active Pension: Asset or Income

Some divorces happen late in life. It's not uncommon for one of the parties to have a pension that is in pay status, meaning he or she is already receiving a monthly pension check. The question can arise as to whether the pension is at least in part (the percentage vested during the marriage) a marital asset, or is it rather a component of the pensioned party's total income. The court, depending on the circumstances of the case, can go either way on this issue.

Often before the pension can become active the pensioned party must notify the pensioning company or agent how the retiring employee wishes to receive the pension. For example, it could be paid out over a fixed period of time or over his or her entire remaining lifetime. It might allow continued payments to the nonpensioned spouse at some reduced level if the pensioned party dies, or maybe not. These selections can be very difficult or even impossible to alter once in place.

Regardless, if the judge's goal is for the nonpensioned party to receive a portion of the pension, he or she will find a way. If there's a possibility to divide up the actual pension, it will probably be treated as an asset. If not, the court may simply allocate to the nonpensioned party an appropriate portion of the pension's income stream in the form of spousal maintenance.

This is a very simplified explanation of a subject that is rather complex due to all the situational possibilities and pension restrictions. The good news is that if the pension is actually being collected, it's much easier to determine its specific value.

401(k)s and IRAs

The preceding discussion dealt with a traditional pension plan. It's often called a defined benefit plan because for a given age, salary, and years of employment there's an exact amount of money that will be paid out. Plans like this used to be the norm, but not any more.

Today, companies are more likely to offer an alternative retirement plan called a 401(k), which has a defined contribution rather than a defined benefit. Every month the employee and the employer contribute specific amounts into this retirement account.

As with the defined benefit plan it's difficult to predict the future value of a 401(k) account since it depends on interest rates, the stock market, the amount contributed, etc. However, it's easy for the court to know the current value of a 401(k) account and to divide up this amount.

So, unlike the situation with a defined benefit plan, the receiving spouse usually doesn't have to wait to get a portion of his or her spouse's 401(k) savings. IRAs and similar kinds of defined contribution plans are dealt with much the same as 401(k) accounts.

When the divorce is final, funds can be rolled over from one spouse's 401(k) plan into the other spouse's 401(k) account or IRA (he or she may need to start one) without paying any penalties or taxes. Of course, if the receiving spouse spends the money rather than rolling it over, it becomes subject to income tax and, if the receiving spouse is less than 59-1/2 years old, a 10% penalty.

However, there's a useful exception to the withdrawal penalty rule if the receiving spouse is under the minimum 59-1/2 age requirement. On a one-time basis, that spouse can use the 401(k) or other company plan to immediately pay off marital debt that's the responsibility of the receiving spouse or for any other purpose. While income taxes will have to be paid, the 10% penalty is avoided. This exception does not apply to a distribution from an IRA. Talk to a tax expert for more information.

Couples wishing to maximize this benefit should structure a plan so that the spouse receiving the 401(k) rollover also gains significant marital debt. Of course, this requires balancing other financial aspects of the divorce to make it a fair deal. That can be done only through an out-of-court negotiation. Don't expect the judge to worry about such intricate tax issues.

Social Security Isn't Property

Unlike a pension, which is normally looked upon as an asset by the court, Social Security benefits are viewed as income. Therefore, the judge is more likely to simply add whatever each spouse receives in Social Security payments (now or in the future) to the rest of that person's projected income.

Then, looking at the total income potential of each party, the court will decide on the money issues of child support, maintenance, and property distribution (to the extent that income affects the asset split).

School Is Cool

There's a special pension that still needs to be discussed. Missouri state legislatures hold our public school teaches in high regard. One demonstration of their special status is that Public School Retirement Pensions are specifically excluded from the property negotiation during a divorce. The court has no power to allocate a portion of this pension to the nonteaching spouse. In fact, it is considered to be the separate property of the person who earned the pension.

The argument for doing this is that teachers don't pay Social Security and therefore the school pension is their only retirement program. This may be true, but it's also true for many federal workers who don't pay for and are not entitled to Social Security. Their pensions have no such protection.

Of course, one of the factors a court considers in dividing the marital property is how much separate property each person has. So the fact that the teacher gets to keep the entire pension may be taken into account in dividing the marital property.

In any event, it isn't a completely free ride. If the pension is already in "pay status"—in other words, if the teacher is already retired and receiving monthly payments—the income derived from the teacher's pension is included when determining each party's responsibilities for child support. It also is used to decide the teaching party's ability to pay or need to receive maintenance.

Stock Options

Some companies like to reward faithful employees by giving them an opportunity to buy stock in the company at a discounted price. These opportunities, known as "stock options," usually can't be exercised unless the employee stays with the company for a certain number of years. Stock options, if they are earned during the marriage, are marital property and need to be considered by the court along with the rest of the marital property.

There are two problems in dealing with these options. First, determining their value is almost impossible. For example, if Emerson Electric gives its employee an option to buy stock at $45 per share and the stock is trading at $50 per share today, we can easily see that the option is worth $5 today, since the employee would immediately gain $5 by buying a share at $45. But the stock market never stands still, and by the time the stock option is vested (available to be used), the stock value may have climbed to $60 or dropped to $30.

Second, stock options are almost never transferable. Only the employee is eligible to exercise the options. So you can't simply say that the nonemployee will receive half of the stock options. To get around this problem lawyers have devised ways of giving the nonemployee the right to require the employee to exercise half of the options. Be sure to discuss this issue with your lawyer if stock options are in your pile of marital assets.

Potpourri Again

Here are a few more odds and ends worth passing along.

If one spouse knowingly wasted significant marital assets (gave extravagant gifts to Suzy Floozy in an extra-marital affair, allowed the house to be foreclosed with loss of equity when he or she could have prevented it, spent a lot of time losing on the casino boats, etc.), a por-tion of the wasted amount may be taken from the waste-ful spouse's asset share and given to the other spouse.

Sometimes an outside party may also have a claim on a marital asset. Let's say two couples jointly buy a sum-mer home. The outside couple needs to officially join the divorce case with respect to this issue so the court can protect their interest in the relevant property. This pro-vides another good reason to settle out of court. Do you really want your brother-in-law or next-door neighbor to be a party to your divorce?

Whether a corporation owned by one of the spouses is marital or separate property will be determined by the court and dealt with accordingly. However, even if it is a marital asset, a judge normally won't divide up a corporate asset and disassemble the entity. Rather, the corporate value and income will be offset in some manner using other assets and income. The exception is when the corporation is merely a tax shell and not a truly functioning business.

Remember that the valuation date of all assets is the trial date. And if there's a retrial, the valuation date becomes the retrial date.

Dotting the I's and Crossing the T's

While the final divorce judgment lays out the division of assets, there's often more work to be done. If lawyers are representing the parties, they will take care of these details. However, when attorneys aren't used, things can slip through a crack or two.

The most common issue relates to the marital home. As mentioned earlier, the court may award the home to one spouse, with the requirement that the equity in the home be equally shared. In order to conclude this transfer of ownership, the spouse keeping the home must receive from the other spouse a "quitclaim deed." In this document the homeless spouse gives up all rights to the marital home in exchange for his or her equity rights as granted in the final judgment.

Failure to get such documents executed right away can create lots of problems later on. Yes, most can be resolved, but usually that involves both added expenses and delays. So before running off into the sunset, make sure any necessary follow-up documents are executed.

Enter the Tax Man

A dollar is not always worth a dollar. Taxes need to be considered when property is being split up. Take a look at the story of three different assets.

The first is a marital home that was purchased 10 years ago for $75,000 and is now appraised at $125,000. The second is a seasonal camp also purchased 10 years ago for $75,000 and is presently worth $125,000. The third asset is a stock investment made less than a year ago. The shares were bought for $25,000 and by some miracle are currently valued at $75,000. Now assume that just after the divorce all three are sold.

The $50,000 capital gain on the house ($125,000 less $75,000) is not taxed by either the federal or Missouri governments since it is within the capital gains limit for a home that was a primary residence for two of the most recent five years. (New laws are making it even easier to avoid this tax for divorcing couples.)

Meanwhile, the $50,000 ($125,000 less $75,000) capital gain on the camp is taxable because it wasn't a primary residence. However, since it was owned for more than a year, the profit is taxed at a low long term capital gain rate. At the time this book was published this rate could not exceed 15%. So in the worst case the tax due would be $7,500.

The $50,000 stock profit ($75,000 less $25,000) made in less than a year is a short term capital gain and gets taxed at the ordinary income rate (the same rate as your salary, etc). Adding the income from this stock sale to the rest of your earned income could result in achieving a substantial federal tax rate. For example, if that rate was 25% (it could be higher or lower), you'd be paying $12,500 in taxes on the stock sale. And both the camp and the stock gains are also subject to Missouri taxes!

Those are shockingly important differences. Shocking to you perhaps, but not to the Missouri court that often ignores them. After all, the judge is trying to balance many factors when putting together a final judgment. He or she isn't just worrying about the IRS.

So if taxes play an important role in the property split, don't leave it up to the court to decide; negotiate a settlement with your spouse. If that's not possible, you'll need to have a tax expert testify at the trial. Of course, it's likely that your spouse will counter this testimony with an expert witness having an opposing viewpoint.

So even after all that expensive talent is paid for, it may still be a guessing game as to what will appear in the final order. The judge could decide on a 50–50 split, but after the taxes are paid it may be hardly that.

Again, We Repeat Ourselves

As was mentioned in other parts of this book, spousal support and property are taxed differently. Maintenance is taxed as ordinary income for the one receiving it (like it was salary). It's a tax deduction for the one who pays the support. Property isn't taxed when it's received, but only when it's sold and often at a lower capital-gains rate.

Therefore, if the receiving party is in a low income tax bracket and the paying spouse is in a high one, it may make sense to pay more spousal support (highly taxed income) and give fewer assets (usually lower taxed income). But a receiving spouse in a high income bracket may prefer to get less support and more assets.

And keep in mind the importance of timing. All asset transfers between the parties are tax free if they're done according to the settlement and completed within one

year of the divorce becoming final. After that, there's a
risk of creating taxable events.

Just in case you've forgotten, the party receiving child
support pays no taxes on it. It's also not a tax deduction
for the paying parent.

Nobody Does It Better

There's little doubt that the best way for the parties to
achieve the most tax effective asset distribution is to do
it themselves. However, tax laws are highly complex
and frequently not at all intuitive. Seek professional tax
assistance. Yes, it's expensive, but the savings will usually more than justify the cost.

CHAPTER 13

Determining Income

Why Income Is So Important

W HEN IT COMES to settling the financial issues of divorce, nothing is more important than the family income. Love, spite, kids, support, and everything else get taken care of only to the extent there is money to do so.

Missouri provides welfare and similar help for those with low incomes and the very rich have few financial problems. However, the majority caught in the middle are left to cut back on everything until the bleeding stops.

Yet there may be more money than you think. Missouri looks well beyond the tax records and makes judgments based on what each party could be earning, should be earning, or is earning but not reporting.

Checking Out the W-2

While the amount indicated on a spouse's most recent income tax form represents a starting point, it isn't necessarily the final figure used by the court. For example, what if the husband was laid off during the year for several months and is now back at work?

If the judge relied only on his latest reported annual income, it would look pretty low. The reverse is also true. Perhaps the husband is in real estate sales and it's been an unusually profitable period. In order to be fair, his income performance over the longer term should be considered, not just the most recent year.

Therefore, a person's earning history for three, four, or even five years, including overtime and bonuses and commissions, is often used to come up with an average income. Based on this calculation the judge develops a reasonable forecast of what each party's future earnings are likely to be.

But sometimes the past doesn't predict the future. Let's say a wife recently got a big promotion or a new job with a huge pay increase. Maybe she just finished law school and is unemployed but interviewing for a position.

Now the court has to look forward to determining the right income to use. What kind of salary, overtime, and bonus is the new posting likely to pay? There are plenty of statistics available to allow for a good estimate.

Besides salary, income includes earnings from rental property, bank deposits, mutual funds, stocks and bonds, etc. It also covers money received through pensions, annuities, and Social Security.

Working "Off the Books" and Other Misadventures

The judge will want to include all cash income as well. The term "cash" often is a substitute for the words "earnings that I don't report to the IRS."

Operating on a cash basis is particularly popular with some handymen and other private businesses. Frequently a person has more unreported income than reported earnings. And don't forget about undisclosed tips.

Part-time earnings can be another source of cash income. This could be money made weekends clearing and splitting trees or by selling hand knitted sweaters at the town market, or from vegetables and other produce sold from the back of the barn.

Noncash transactions are also considered to be income in Missouri. For example, a Steelville farm hand who gets free housing as part of his job will have the rental value of the accommodations plus the amount of free heat and electricity added to his earnings. The same goes for the personal use of a company car that a salesman or executive might receive.

Barter payments represent another type of noncash earnings. In such transactions someone does something like paint a house in exchange for being given an almost new all-terrain vehicle. One-time events won't mean much to the court, but there are people who conduct a large part of their working activities using barter.

And Still More Money

One profitable area for the other party's lawyer to explore is the self-employed spouse who earns a mere $8,000 a year, yet magically affords a Corvette, a golf club membership, a large house in Ladue, and a four bedroom "cabin" with a view at the Lake of the Ozarks.

It's often possible to get the court to "impute"—that is, to attribute to him or her—an income based on this miracle worker being employed by a local corporation at a salary well beyond $8,000 (see "Everything is Not Enough" below).

But it can be even more profitable to rework the business' income statement in a way that shows how the poorly paid owner is really earning $200,000 a year, and that based on this "real" income, the business is worth $2 million instead of the claimed value of $100,000.

The Spy Who Loved You

Go to court thinking you can hide this extra income and you'll most likely be disappointed. Remember, your spouse knows or at least suspects what's been going on, and his or her attorney has seen it all before. So guess who's going to spill the beans to the judge.

To help things along, each spouse has the right to receive copies of the other's tax returns and business records. It's important that these documents provide an accurate earnings picture. Judges take an immediate dislike to anyone presenting false or misleading information.

A word of caution here may be useful. Spouses who expose their better half's unreported or underreported income may get caught themselves. In all likelihood the "bean spilling spouse" signed the income tax forms for the years in question. If he or she knew that the reported income was false, both spouses may have committed a fraud. The IRS has significant penalties for such actions, including all expense paid "vacations." Discuss these possibilities with a lawyer.

Everything Is Not Enough

By now you realize that the income calculations for divorce purposes can be quite different from those submitted to the tax authorities. But how much gets reported as earnings or even what is actually earned isn't always the measure of total income.

The court's definition of income is a person's ability to support him- or herself on a best efforts basis, as well as, if necessary, to contribute to the support of the children and the other spouse. The IRS may have a different one, but that's not important.

If either party has the realistic possibility of significantly improving his or her earning power by altering work activities (change employer or type of work or simply start working), the court will consider that spouse to be "voluntarily underemployed." So even when a party is totally honest about what he or she earns, that may not be good enough.

A common example of this situation is the self-employed professional or craftsman who earns substantially less than could be earned by doing the same job for a corporation or general contractor. Another example is when a previously well compensated executive decides to "drop out" and takes up a lower income producing activity.

In these situations the court first determines if it's likely suitable higher paying jobs are actually available (usually through expert testimony presented by the other party). If they are, the court will assume the higher income level (referred to as "imputed income") for all support calculations. The judge can't force the easygoing spouse to take the better paid position, but the amount of child support and maintenance (alimony) specified in the final order may leave little choice.

The stay-at-home mom or dad can also be an example of an underemployed spouse. Once the kids are of school age, Missouri courts generally assume that the unemployed parent is choosing not to work.

Therefore, an income for that spouse may be imputed by the court. The amount of assumed earnings is based on the spouse's previous work history, any special training or skills he or she has, and the local job market.

The court is always optimistic. It believes that almost everyone is employable. So unless there's a limiting medical problem or an issue of an equally serious nature, such as having to care for a chronically ill child, it's pretty hard for the stay-at-home parent to avoid getting assigned some amount of income.

In summary, the fact that a spouse prefers to study French literature instead of continuing to captain a 747 airliner is of no concern to a Missouri judge. The state's point of view is that he or she should have thought of the consequences before entering into matrimony.

A Friend in Need

Other people's money can sometimes enter into the income calculation. That's because the court has the right to consider "all resources available to a spouse" when determining a party's ability to pay or need to receive maintenance.

So if a lover is living with one of the parties, the contribution the lover is or should be making to the payment of the divorced spouse's expenses will be taken into consideration. Similarly, the judge may add the value of the rent paid to one of the parties by a relative sharing a home with a former spouse, even if no rent or expenses are actually paid by the relative. Generally, these situations are not at play during the divorce process. They are much more common after the divorce when one side is seeking to modify a payment.

Child support is a different matter. Only the income of the two parents is considered. Even if a parent has remarried, a stepparent's income is never considered in determining the amount of child support to be paid by both legal parents. However, if the parent decides to stop working simply because the new spouse makes enough money to support both of them, the court will still assume that the newly unemployed parent is earning what he or she used to earn.

Don't Count Assets

One thing that isn't income is property. For example, if a spouse has rental property, don't expect the court to count the value of that asset when considering the party's ability to pay monthly maintenance. Also, the judge won't give some of that rental property to the spouse needing the maintenance in order to reduce or eliminate the monthly maintenance payment coming from the other side.

The asset split is strictly based on the process outlined in the property distribution chapters. However, once the split is determined, any income generated by the assets retained by a party (like interest income, dividends, rental income, etc.) is, of course, included when determining a spouse's total income.

The Final Twist

Spousal support is income to the person who gets it. So the judge will add the maintenance payment to the receiving spouse's income before doing the child support calculation. At the same time, this maintenance payment gets subtracted from the income of the paying party before making the same calculation.

CHAPTER 14

Divorce Strategies and Issues

It Takes Two to Tangle

A STRONG MESSAGE runs throughout this book. A fair-minded couple with the assistance, as required, of lawyers, mediators, accountants, appraisers, child agencies, etc., is in the best position to reach a satisfactory conclusion.

Destructive behavior is destined to send the emotional life of the family members down the toilet right along with their finances. Yet even when both sides understand the danger, many get caught in the flushing whirlpool.

Each party feels the other is being "totally unreasonable," that the other spouse refuses to be "realistic." His or her ideas are simply "nuts." "How could anyone think that way?"

A True Story About Japan and Baseball

This is a good time to tell a true sports story.

Several years ago an American athlete was playing baseball for a Japanese team when his son became gravely ill.

206

Brain surgery was required, with his survival uncertain. So the American player immediately flew to the US to be with the boy for the operation.

That's when all hell broke loose.

His Japanese teammates, the Japanese media, and the average citizen of Japan was completely outraged. It was beyond their comprehension how such a valuable player could leave the team in the middle of the season. One Japanese player exclaimed, "If my mother was on her deathbed, I would never leave the team."

The reaction in the United States was just the opposite. No one understood the apparently heartless attitude of the Japanese. After all, the man's son was close to death. It seemed the Japanese don't love their families as we do in America. There could be no other reasonable explanation.

Let's stop the story for a moment. Does any of this remind you of talking to your spouse? Two sides miles apart and each positive the other is completely wrong. Is there really only one reasonable way of looking at things? Now back to the story.

As Americans, we believe that the right thing to do in this situation was obvious. So how did the Japanese explain their feelings? Well, it was obvious to them as well.

A Japanese ballplayer knows his family loves him. But his teammates don't love him the way his family does. The other players would never forgive him if he left. So it's his family's love that allows a Japanese player to maintain his obligation to the team.

Clearly, a huge cultural issue was at work here. However, the story makes an important point. There is more than one way of looking at virtually any situation. It's possible for two honorable people to disagree and for both of them to be right based on their legitimate needs and motivations.

If you feel your spouse is being unreasonable, try to see the situation from his or her point of view. Don't let these differences prevent the two of you from finding a meaningful resolution. Remember, men are from Mars and women are from Venus.

Also, keep in mind the consequences of not working out an agreement. Then everything gets left up to the lawyers and the judges. God only knows what planets they're all from!

The Evildoer

But sometimes if it walks like a duck, and quacks like a duck, it's a duck. There are spouses with less than honorable intentions. A weaker spouse may see divorce as an opportunity to establish an early retirement nest egg. Or perhaps just the opposite is true. The spouse with the great job and the greater prospects wants to avoid his or her responsibilities toward the more dependent partner.

Too often the good spouse believes that by being reasonable, the other side will be reasonable too. So he or she makes a fair settlement offer that the evil spouse rejects out of hand. Then, without the evildoer making a counterproposal, the good spouse sends an even more attractive revision. That is also quickly rejected.

If the evil one does make a proposal, it's usually so outrageous that it has no meaning. Still believing that a compromise is possible, the good spouse faxes back counterproposals to these preposterous solutions, where they disappear into the vacuum of the evildoer's cold, cold heart. A one-sided negotiation is a fool's game.

Sometimes the situation is as clear as the one just described. Often it's more subtle. One party is providing reasonable offers, and the other side is discussing them and suggesting alternatives. It looks like progress is being made. However, the other side puts nothing in writing.

Any proposal not in writing is less than worthless. Consider the cost of such wasted negotiations if mediators and lawyers get involved. Refuse to be manipulated in such a manner.

A Lesson in the Art of War

So, if after reading the Japanese baseball story, you still believe that your spouse is up to no good in the negotiation, then it's time to take greater control. Lamar's favorite son, Harry S. Truman, once told us, "Carry the battle to them. Don't let them bring it to you."

"Give'em hell Harry" was right. In war the most important objective is to control the time and place of the battle. That may mean running down to the courthouse as fast as your attorney can schedule the trial, or it may mean just the opposite.

Time for another sports analogy!

In basketball, especially against a stronger team, the greatest danger is to allow the game to be played at the opponent's desired tempo. If a run-and-gun fast-break pace is their preference, then the weaker side has to find a way to slow things down. If the stronger team likes a more leisurely half court game, the other team needs to force the action.

Divorce works much the same. By taking the uncooper-
ative spouse out of his or her comfort zone you gain
greater control of the process. Talk over the possibility of
following this strategy with your lawyer.

Such a manipulative approach is being recommended
only when the other side exhibits destructive behavior.
Do it when the other party is honestly trying to cooperate (cooperating doesn't necessarily mean agreeing to
everything you want), and then you become the destructive spouse.

In summary, maintaining a false hope that the other
spouse by some miracle will see the light is far worse
than having no hope. Take charge of your situation.

Sometimes Things Are Too Comfortable

Another recommendation of this book is to err on the
side of generosity when it comes to temporary payments. However, it shouldn't be done blindly. If there's
any doubt about the cooperative attitude of the other
party, it's better to keep these temporary amounts in line
with what's likely to appear in the final judgment.

That's because an excessively favorable temporary deal,
whether agreed to by the parties or imposed by the judge
in the PDL orders, can kill the receiving spouse's incen-
tive to move toward a possibly less generous final resolution. In fact, the comfortable spouse often works to
slow the process down. Meanwhile, as things drag on,
the judge begins to believe that the paying spouse would
have no problem continuing such ample payments on a
permanent basis.

This slowdown can be accomplished in many imaginative ways. A favorite is for the delaying party to stretch
out the negotiations by always making success appear to

be just around the corner. When the other party catches on to this game, the comfortable spouse may suddenly demand additional or revised data.

For example, he or she now wants the appraisals redone because too much time has passed even though it's unlikely the values have changed. Not surprisingly, the appraiser is backlogged for several weeks.

Another way to extend the process is by requesting a substantial amount of court time to present the case. If one of the parties demands a three or four day trial it's certain to set things back while everyone waits for a large space in the court calendar to become available. Then he or she may get "sick" on the day of the trial or change lawyers just before the big event.

The judge will eventually realize what's going on and put a foot down, but initially the benefit of the doubt is given. Meanwhile, six months or even more can go by.

And Sometimes It Is the Lawyer

Not all lawyers are helpful. While the large majority work to resolve issues in a fair and equitable manner, some may lead their clients astray. Attorneys who put "stars" in the eyes of their clients by making them believe that they can "have it all" do everyone a disservice.

The demanding party becomes certain that the other spouse should be giving more or getting less depending on the situation. Why? Because his or her lawyer says so.

The cost of maintaining an unrealistic attitude is easily measured by counting the extra billing hours of all the lawyers and other professionals who will be forced to get involved. The emotional price is high as well.

So make it clear that you want your attorney to be an "agent of reality." Insist he or she provide a realistic appraisal of the situation. Indicate as well the relationship you desire to have with your spouse after it's all over. A scorched-earth take-no-prisoners approach may be thrilling, but it's hard for the children, or their parents, to thrive on such a barren landscape after the divorce.

Who's Paying for It All

It's no secret that divorces cost money. If the issues are contentious, the amount can become really substantial. And who's expected to pay for it all?

That isn't a difficult question for the couple with ample liquid assets (cash and near cash). But for many it's a serious concern.

Generally, a judge prefers to let each side pay its own fees. But if there's a significant disparity in wealth, the judge will often have the richer spouse provide the poorer one a fixed amount to cover anticipated legal costs. If this money runs out, a top up may be ordered.

To avoid this imposition, the richer spouse should try to negotiate things with the other spouse in advance of the court's decision. Lawyers, who (just like you) enjoy being paid on time, will gladly facilitate this discussion.

One solution is to agree to pay both sides' legal fees from the marital assets. That way each spouse ends up paying only in proportion to the marital asset division.

Negotiation also allows for the possibility of a more imaginative structure. Perhaps, instead of paying the other's legal costs, a better-off spouse is willing to give some additional assets in the settlement. Maybe the poor spouse would rather have those assets and borrow the attorney's fees from friends or family. Judges will not be so creative.

Should the poorer spouse carelessly overspend on lawyers, etc., the judge can balance things out in the final judgment by awarding the richer spouse more of the marital assets. Of course, if the rich spouse's wild legal spending forces the poor spouse to do the same, the judge will make sure the poor spouse gets enough funds from the rich one to stay competitive.

If neither side has money, the spouses should be eager to keep things simple and to reach a settlement with as little fanfare as possible. Hopefully.

Patience Is a Virtue

In a cooperative divorce the overall system works pretty well. But if one party decides to disrupt the process, it can move at a snail's pace.

Most people react poorly to delay. As things drag on, frustration increases. This lowers expectations and weakens the resolve necessary to get an equitable settlement. The frustrated spouse is often put in a nearly impossible financial and emotional position.

There's no simple solution to this headache. If you live and breathe your divorce 24 hours a day, any slowdown will feel two or three times longer than the actual delay. Do the best you can with your attorney's help to stabilize the situation. Then find an activity to take some of your attention away from the misery.

Try learning a new language, take up tennis, plant a garden, or volunteer at a nursing home (nursing homes have a way of putting your problems in perspective!).

Don't ignore the divorce process. That's a good way of losing control. But overcontrolling it can have a similar result. Patience is a certainly a virtue during times like these.

Use Only in Case of Emergency

Sometimes things can't wait. Sometimes the situation is not only frustrating, but really dangerous. Negotiating a resolution isn't an option. It's time for a different strategy. Missouri's Adult Abuse and Child Protection Acts are designed to react quickly to situations involving the abuse or threat of abuse of an adult or a child.

Abuse is defined under this act as any assault, battery, coercion, harassment, sexual assault, or unlawful imprisonment with respect to an adult. For a child (under 18 years old) it includes physical injury, sexual abuse, or emotional abuse.

Naturally, this book's focus is on one spouse abusing the other or their children. But for readers who may have different fish to fry, please note that all stalkers fall under this law as well. It also covers any immediate family or household member.

A household member is a relative or former relative (following a divorce) who currently resides in the same house as the victim or who resided there in the past. It can also be an adult who has been in a continuing romantic or intimate relationship with the victim, or an adult who had a child with the victim, whether or not they ever lived together.

The entire process is designed for speed and effect. While often helpful, a lawyer isn't necessary to gain relief. The circuit clerk is required to assist the victim or the adult representing a child victim.

The first step is to fill out a petition (not a divorce petition, but a special form that the court clerk can provide) setting out the facts in the case. Within a few hours (sometimes within a few minutes) of the petition being filed, a judge will review the document. If the situation is urgent, normal "due process" is bypassed and the judge instructs the sheriff to immediately serve an "*ex parte* order of protection." This usually requires that the dangerous party leave the house. In addition, the fearful spouse is given custody of the children and sole use of the family home, at least until a hearing can be held.

The term "*ex parte*" (pronounced "ex par-tay") means the order is based only on the facts in the petition. The accused (called the "respondent") had no chance to provide a defense. So, within 15 days following the *ex parte* order there must be a hearing where both sides get to present their case.

Of course, if the judge reviews the petition at the time it's filed and feels that the situation isn't urgent, things proceed in a more orderly manner. Rather than issuing an immediate *ex parte* order, a summons is issued requiring the respondent to appear at a hearing to answer to the charges.

Regardless of which process is used, if at the hearing the petition is found to be true, the court will grant a "full order of protection." It lasts between 180 days and one year (usually one year) and can be renewed two times, with each renewal lasting up to a year.

In addition to its protection aspects, the full order of protection can grant the complaining spouse custody of the children and use of the family home and other assets. It may also order the respondent to make maintenance (if the petitioner and the respondent are married) and child support (regardless of whether they are married) payments. Miscellaneous costs, like court fees and other expenses, may be charged to the respondent as well.

But judges don't want an adult abuse order to be an alternative to getting a divorce. The focus is on securing the safety of the petitioning spouse and the children. Therefore, if the court knows a divorce is on the way, decisions on support payments and child custody usually get delayed until the temporary hearing related to the divorce.

Important Advice

All this represents a very serious situation for the respondent. After the final order of protection is issued, any violations are considered criminal misdemeanors that often result in arrest and prosecution. Frequently, the perpetrator will lose firearm privileges.

Equally important, severe limits will be placed on the respondent's ability to contact the petitioning spouse and the children. Physical custody may be supervised or out of the question, depending on the type of abuse involved.

Therefore, if the respondent is indeed guilty or in a position that is difficult to defend, a "consent order" is often the best solution. Under a consent order, the respondent agrees to stay away from the petitioner or the children but doesn't admit any guilt. Given this alternative, the court will not find fault with the respondent.

Unfortunately, unscrupulous petitioners (sometimes knowingly supported by their attorneys) may seek an unfounded protection order to simply force the other spouse out of the house or to gain other leverage in the divorce. If someone is unfairly accused of abuse, it's very important that he or she fights and wins the case at the hearing. Once a spouse is found culpable and removed from the family, it's extremely difficult to regain the rights lost under the order.

Please note that it's a criminal act on the part of the petitioner (the one accusing the other spouse of abuse) to misrepresent the facts on the petition. There's also the possibility of a civil lawsuit by the respondent (the one being accused of abuse) for damages if such misrepresentation can be proven.

Children Should Be Off Limits

Wars have rules, too. During the divorce process a good rule is to keep the children out of the argument. Unfortunately, this doesn't always hold true.

One parent may attempt to turn the children against the other. Perhaps it's just spite or to enhance a negotiating position. Maybe he or she believes it's a way to gain greater custody. These strategies usually backfire, with the results being the exact opposite of what was intended.

Unfortunately, there's no quick fix when a spouse uses the children to manipulate his or her situation. The best approach may be to seek a temporary restraining order, but this is fairly unusual.

Nevertheless, such actions may eventually catch up with the falsely complaining party. The court takes a dim view of a parent who sets a child against the other parent. Remember, when making the final parenting decision, a judge will consider the desire and ability of each parent to foster in the child a positive relationship with the other parent.

A Motorbike in the Basement

Even when each side shows reasonable respect for the other, issues can come up that unnecessarily derail the situation. Such was the case with a Cross Timbers wife in the process of dividing up the more trivial assets of the marriage.

Her soon to be ex-husband had a little motorbike that he wanted to keep. At first the wife agreed, but later on she changed her mind and dug in her heels. No way was she going to have their young boy riding that "death machine" every time he spent the night with his father. She demanded to get that motorbike asset, which she then planned to sell "real quick." The befuddled Cross Timbers husband dug his heels in too.

Of course, the fact being ignored by both sides was that the husband could easily buy another motorbike, perhaps an even larger, faster one. So, as is often the case, a minor issue became a major one while the entire divorce process got set on its ear for quite some time. More delay, more money, and more bad feelings.

So what happened to the motorbike? It doesn't matter, because this story has nothing to do with the motorbike. It's all about losing control over one's life (and the life of the soon to be ex-spouse). It's about standing on the edge of something new and being afraid to jump.

Most divorces have a "motorbike in the basement" of one kind or another. There's always something that represents moving from a stable life (despite its faults) to an unknown existence. While the fear it generates may not be totally irrational, it's almost always counterproductive.

So before going off the deep end, make sure it's worth the delay, cost, and effort. Using a military metaphor, ask yourself, "Is this a hill to die for?"

The Ultimate Tactic

The ideal strategy is to have both sides working together toward a fair settlement. Remember, children are only as happy as their least happy parent.

And yes, your life is about to change.

CHAPTER 15

The Perils of Living Together

Life in the Center Lane

MISSOURI IS FAMOUS for its Midwest orientation and Bible Belt status. Together these perceptions speak of a "do it by the rules" and "keep both feet on the ground" mindset.

Well that's how we like to see ourselves anyway. The truth is that while the Show-Me State's character may not be in the fast lane of nontraditional lifestyles, it is definitely picking up speed.

This seems certainly true when it comes to cohabitation. Many couples prefer to skip the getting married formality and rush right into living together. Together they buy cars, borrow money, have lots of children, and even own a house, but they just never get hitched.

Time alone is said to resolve many issues, but not everything. Common law marriage doesn't exist in Missouri. A guy and a gal can share room and board for 50 years and they are still not legally married until they say officially "I do."

So what happens when Rosie and Phil, a Fountain N' Lakes couple that has lived together for 15 years, decide to break up? Just as with divorcing spouses, the best approach is for them to work out an acceptable settlement on their own. One thing neither can do is file a divorce petition. Divorces are for married customers only.

In fact, none of the maintenance and property distribution laws that protect married partners apply to live-together couples. That's because live-together relationships are viewed as partnerships, not much different from the accounting firm down the street. It's strictly a business deal.

The one big difference is that the accountants are likely to have a partnership agreement that spells out the rights of the parties. You can bet your Chiefs season tickets that Phil and Rosie have very little in writing.

Living Together with the Kids

One thing that's the same regardless of a couple's marriage status is how the kid issues get handled. In general, things involving the children (support, custody, etc.) work just as they do in the divorce process. You can find more detailed information on the children issues in the relevant chapters of this book. Grandparents should also review the chapter on grandparental rights.

Lee Marvin Should Have Lived in Missouri

Some time ago, the late actor Lee Marvin made the term "palimony" famous. Lee lived for many years with a woman who claimed to have given up her career to keep the home fires burning. Eventually they split and Lee was sued for palimony.

Palimony is essentially a monthly payment made by one live-together partner to the other after they go their separate ways. The legal argument is that a couple sharing bed and board for an extended period of time establish a long term commitment to each other just the same as married folks do. The palimony payment is the not-married crowd's version of spousal support.

While there have been some large palimony awards, Mr. Marvin basically won this high-profile case when the woman was granted a trivial support payment. Later on, the lady ended up with Dick Van Dyke, the pride of West Plains, MO, but that's a different story.

Back in Fountain N' Lakes, Phil is also looking forward to collecting some palimony. It seems that Rosie was the ambitious partner and started a successful Missouri cuisine bakery named Cake of the Ozarks. Phil, meanwhile, wasn't employed, preferring to take care of the home and the children.

He speaks often of sacrificing his personal career for Rosie's jelly roll success. He also claims to have contributed half the money to start the business. Now, as the "dough" rolls in, he feels entitled to some kind of maintenance payment following the breakup.

Of course, if Phil had been married to Rosie those long 15 years, he might have gotten his meal ticket punched. After all, with divorce the judge takes into account the contributions of the stay-at-home spouse. But in this case they were only living together. There's no palimony in Missouri.

Dividing Up Live-Together Property

Phil's biggest surprise comes when he discovers how the assets will be divided. Equitable distribution, where separate property stays separate and the judge allocates marital property like a state-sponsored Robin Hood, is only for divorcing couples. When live-together partners break up, the process is more similar to collapsing a business entity.

Phil, having supplied half the initial $50,000 Cake of the Ozarks investment, went to court demanding 50% of the business' current $350,000 value. In such a case, the first thing the judge will do is review any relevant agreements existing between the couple.

This might be a general live-together agreement that spells out how assets are shared if things go south (similar to a pre- or postnuptial agreement). Or it could be one that focuses on a specific asset like the bakery (a partnership agreement). If there's nothing in writing, the court figures it out the best it can.

You'll recall that in a divorce, where the money came from is a key element when determining property rights. In a live-together property settlement, the name on an account, deed, title, loan, registration, agreement, etc., means everything. The source of those assets isn't nearly as important.

For example, if during their live-together relationship Rosie put $60,000 of her earnings into a bank account that was only in her name, that money would belong to her alone. But if she and Phil had been married during that same period, those earnings would be marital assets even though Phil's name wasn't on the account. In that case, Phil would have had a good chance of the divorce judgment passing along some of that account's balance to him.

Back to the lemon meringue palace. It seems that all the documents related to the bakery are only in Rosie's name. That includes the deed to the building, the receipts for its furnishings, and the bank accounts. There's also no written business or live-together agreement between Rosie and Phil. "Two people in love don't need agreements," he remembers her saying. So the only item with Phil's name on it is his check to Rosie for $25,000 covering half the start-up costs.

Another important factor the judge will note is that Phil never worked directly for Cake of the Ozarks. In other words, nothing he did led directly to its success.

Given such circumstances, the court could decide that Phil isn't a half owner of the cake factory but rather just a creditor or maybe not even that.

So in this case he doesn't get $175,000 (half of the $350,000 appraised value). Instead, the judge orders Rosie to repay Phil the $25,000 he "loaned" her along with interest. Rosie keeps the $350,000 asset and Phil's really unhappy.

Becoming an "Honest" Man and Woman

Now let's explore what happens if a live-together couple eventually gets married and then files for divorce. Even when many years of cohabitation are followed by only a very short marriage (not so uncommon), the divorcing parties still get the full monty when it comes to partaking in Missouri's divorce laws. That's a significant difference from the live-together situation where the couple is treated more like a business partnership.

Assume that Cake of the Ozarks was started while Phil and Rosie were living together. Later on they got married and the marriage lasted 15 years.

The court is still likely to consider the bakery Rosie's alone, because it was started prior to the marriage (separate property) and everything is in Rosie's name. But any money Rosie earns from the bakery during the marriage is definitely a marital property.

Also, the judge realizes that Phil is unlikely to ever achieve a high paying career, while Rosie is in a position to continue making a substantial income after the divorce. So Phil might get spousal support. After all, he is nearing retirement age and will need an asset or income base to help him live. Phil is finally happy.

The key factor is that at some point Phil and Rosie got married.

What Does All This Have to Do with You

Some readers may wonder why a chapter on living together is in a book about divorce. They are in the minority. The majority knows why.

While there are no official statistics, it's clear that many spouses are into their next relationship well before the divorce is granted. After the final judgment newly divorced parties often prefer not to rush into marriage again. They'd rather come and go as they please.

But that doesn't mean there aren't risks. In fact, they can often be greater than those existing in a marriage. The stay-at-home mom or dad in a live-together situation who ignores these risks can be in for a big surprise if it all comes crashing down. No job, no maintenance, no pension sharing, maybe not even the house or car if these things are only in the other partner's name. Pretty much not much at all. The working partner or one who carelessly brings assets into the relationship is taking risks too.

So live-together situations need to be run like a business.

- Keep assets in the name of the party who owns them.

- Keep loans in the name of the party who benefits from them.

- Joint assets should be in both parties' names.

- Have a written agreement that clearly outlines how joint properties and loans will be divided if the relationship ends.

- If you're staying home to care for the children while the other party works, put in writing a support plan that gets implemented if things fall apart.

As St. Joseph native Walter Cronkite would say, "And that's the way it is."

APPENDIX

Summary of Missouri's Divorce Process
(shown in the usual order of occurrence)

Petition—One party prepares a petition. The petitioner's lawyer files the petition with the Circuit Court, usually along with a financial statement. If the petitioner doesn't have a lawyer he or she prepares and files the petition directly with the Circuit Court.

Service of Summons—If both sides have lawyers, the attorney preparing the petition contacts the other party's lawyer, who normally agrees to a "waiver of necessity of service"; alternatively, a sheriff or private process server is utilized. If lawyers are not involved, the court arranges for the sheriff to deliver the petition to the other party. If the location of the other spouse is unknown, a notice is run in a local newspaper for three weeks.

Answer—The respondent (the spouse receiving the petition) is expected to formally reply to the petition within 30 days, either admitting or denying what is stated in the petition (referred to as an "answer"). The respondent's lawyer will file the answer with the court, usually along with a financial statement, and send a copy to the petitioner's attorney. If lawyers are not involved, the respondent follows the same procedure except that in addition to filing it with the court, a copy of the answer is sent directly to the petitioner. If the respondent fails to provide an answer, the petitioner can have a default hearing (uncontested hearing) and a final judgment will be issued.

Parenting Plan—A plan for managing the children issues (legal and physical custody, child support, dispute resolution) must be submitted within 30 days of the respondent receiving the petition. The parties can submit separate plans or they can agree to a joint one. The plan may be temporary (until the divorce is finalized) or permanent (if both sides agree).

Pendente Lite **Order (PDL)**—If the parties cannot agree on temporary issues such as the parenting plan, child support, and maintenance, a PDL hearing is held and the judge will issue a PDL order (temporary order) covering the unresolved issues. This temporary order stays in effect until the final judgment is decided.

Parental Education Class—Within 45 days of filing the divorce petition, parents with minor children must attend a court-sponsored class that provides training on how to reduce the trauma of divorce on the children.

Discovery—Either party can request information related to the divorce from the other party under oath (interrogatories, depositions, request for production of documents, etc.) and can obtain statements and documents from third parties.

Settlement Conference—A meeting of the parties and their lawyers with the judge is held in the judge's chambers to inform the court what progress is being made toward reaching a settlement agreement. If the parties feel they cannot reach agreement, a trial date will be set. Normally there are between one and four such conferences.

Settlement Agreement—A divorce agreement reached by the parties that eliminates the need to go to trial. It is submitted to the court for approval at a noncontested hearing or through the submission of affidavits. This is also known as a "separation agreement" or a "marital settlement agreement" or sometimes an "MSA."

Trial—A trial is held to address all divorce issues that the parties cannot reach agreement on.

Final Judgment—The ultimate decree by the court itemizes all the final provisions pertaining to the children, maintenance, and the division of assets and debts. The decree may be based upon the parties' settlement agreement, or in the event the parties cannot reach an agreement, the decree will be the decision of the judge after hearing evidence from both parties at a trial. It becomes final 30 days after being issued and any request for changes or corrections must be made prior to its becoming final.

Posttrial Appeals and Motions to Modify—A party can appeal the final order due to an abuse of discretion on the part of the judge or because the decision was not consistent with the law or the evidence. From time to time following the issuance of the final judgment, a party can request that the court alter the final judgment based on a change in circumstances (a motion to modify). Changes are normally limited to child support, child custody, and spousal support. The asset distribution is rarely changed following the divorce decree becoming final.

Diagram of Missouri's Divorce Process

Note: The following chart gives a general outline of the sequence of events. However, depending on the specific situation, the process can vary.

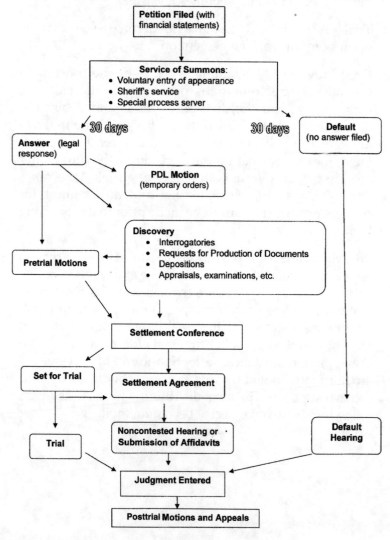

Things You'll Need to Bring to Your Lawyer

A. List of Questions You Have Regarding Your Divorce and the Divorce Process

B. Income Information
1. Tax returns and all IRS forms related to the returns (joint and separate) for at least three years
2. Private business tax returns (if any) for at least three years
3. Pay stubs for both spouses for last four months

C. Property Information
1. Real estate owned
   - mortgages and notes
   - names of owners
   - deeds
   - assessment notices
   - closing statements
   - source of down payments and purchase prices
   - appraisal reports
2. Vehicles owned (cars, tractors, four-wheelers, boats, personal watercraft)
   - year, make, and model
   - debt, monthly payments, creditor
   - blue book value
3. Bank accounts and stocks and bonds
   - statements showing value
   - date of purchase and source of funds
4. Pensions, 401(k), IRA, etc.
   - plan description
   - statements showing valuation both currently and at the time of the marriage
5. Life insurance policies (especially those with cash value)
   - statement showing value

6. Farm equipment and livestock
   - statement showing value
7. Other significant assets (art collections, sports memorabilia, antiques, time share, royalties, patents, etc.)
   - description and value of each asset (appraisal reports)
   - location of the assets
   - date of purchase and source of funds

D. Other Debts
1. Credit card debt
   - credit card numbers
   - account ownership (joint or separate)
   - list of items charged
   - debt owed (current statement)
2. Installment debt/student loans
   - name of debtor
   - purpose of debt
   - amount and terms

E. Family Information
1. Marriage information
   - names, dates of birth, and Social Security numbers of the spouses
   - date of marriage
   - date of separation
   - prenuptial agreements (agreements made before the marriage)
   - postnuptial agreements (agreements made during the marriage)
   - separation agreements, mediation agreements
   - outline of any other arrangements (written or not written) regarding the separation, such as support payments, child support, etc.
   - medical information
     —special requirements and conditions
     —medical/dental insurance source and cost

2. Children information
   • names, dates of birth, and Social Security numbers
   • school issues
       —name and address of schools
       —teachers' names
       —grades and general performance
   • special activities (religion, camps, sports, music, etc.)
   • special needs (medical/medication, tutors, braces, etc.)
   • pediatrician's name/address (include any other regularly seen doctors)
   • daycare provider
       —name/address
       —weekly and annual cost
3. Other legal documents
   • prior divorces of either spouse
       —divorce dates and copies of the decrees
   • other court documents regarding issues of family abuse or criminal activity
   • probate papers, guardianships, trusts
   • any significant lawsuits, worker's compensation claims
   • Social Security status and payments if any received by either spouse
4. Marriage time line
   • Create an outline of all important marriage events (both good and bad), starting with the marriage itself and continuing on in the order they occurred right up until the present day. If the parties lived together for a long period of time, it is useful to start from the time of living together. Things listed in this time line will include the marriage date, employment and related changes (promotions, salary increases, unemployment periods), legal events, birth of children, reallocations, serious medical events, the separation, etc.

5. Typical family life
  • give a brief description of typical life of the family (use
    actual events for examples)
    —school day
    —weekend
    —vacation

Things to Do After the Divorce

1. Get a certified copy of the divorce decree (your lawyer can do this).
2. Retrieve important original documents given to the lawyers during the divorce.
   1. deeds
   2. tax documents and pay stubs
   3. photos
3. Change all loans, mortgages, and credit cards to the name of the party who is responsible for the debt. If the names cannot be removed at the time of the divorce, follow up every six months to see if the situation has changed.
4. Record deeds in the name of the party who owns the property.
5. Change the names on relevant insurance policies (auto, home, etc.).
6. Change the beneficiary on life insurance, pensions, 401(k) plans, IRAs.
7. Provide proper notification of a Qualified Domestic Relationship Order (QDRO) to the pension plan administrator if appropriate.
8. Notify your health insurance company of the reduction in family members covered or, if you were covered by your spouse's policy, check into your COBRA rights or secure alternative insurance.
9. Alter your will to reflect the changes brought on by the divorce.
10. Change the names on automobile registrations and titles.
11. If it was a high-conflict case, maintain a confidential journal of the children's visits, activities, and other significant events.

12. Register the divorce with the proper agencies if you move to another state.

13. If you are receiving child support, notify your former spouse when each child is no longer eligible for child support.

14. Keep track of all child support and maintenance paid or received and keep a ledger of all expenses for the children that are required to be divided between you and your former spouse.

Telephone and Computer Do's and Don'ts

Whether it's the old-fashioned hard-wired type or the latest cell model, everyone uses the telephone. E-mails, text messaging, and the Internet are also major methods of communication. All these activities leave trails that are easy to follow. And don't think that hitting a computer's delete button is the answer. Deleted messages can be picked up from your hard drive.

If you share a computer with your spouse, assume that he or she will have access to all your computer activities. Can these be submitted in court? It depends, but regardless it will give the other party a lot of confidential information. And using a shared computer to communicate with your lawyer may void the attorney-client privilege. In other words the court will assume that you didn't consider the information given your lawyer to be confidential.

Experience shows that given cause, the court is usually willing to issue a subpoena allowing a spouse to obtain the other spouse's telephone records.

This is serious stuff. So follow some simple rules if the above possibilities are a cause for concern.

1. Remember that the telephone company keeps a record of every call you make. For sensitive numbers use a public phone.

2. Change the passwords on your computer and cell phone to ones your spouse doesn't know and can't guess.

3. Don't put sensitive information in e-mails. Service providers may keep copies of these e-mails and they can be subpoenaed.

4. **Assume every e-mail you write will be evidence in a trial.** Read your e-mail before you hit the send button and be sure you haven't written anything you will regret later.

5. Watch out for chat rooms and embarrassing websites. Often what you say and/or see can be traced to you.

6. Make sure your computer doesn't contain software that tracks your activities.

7. Don't listen in on or record your spouse's or children's telephone calls.

8. Don't access any computer, voice mail, or cell phone that is not in your name.

9. Don't keep important information only on your computer. Some of it may go missing due to either your spouse or simply an electronic gremlin. Always have a separate backup.

Index

Meet the Authors

Alan Freed

For over 25 years, Alan Freed has guided Missourians through the difficult straits of divorce, while establishing himself as one of Missouri's leaders in the fields of mediation and collaborative divorce. A 1983 graduate of the Washington University School of Law, Alan has practiced in Clayton for his entire career. He became a member of the law firm of Paule, Camazine & Blumenthal, P.C. at its founding in 1994.

Alan's contributions to the legal community include working as an adjunct professor at the Washington University School of Law, and as the author of *Appellate Practice*, Second Edition (with Daniel P. Card II), in the Missouri Practice series, and of "Mediation and Other Forms of Alternative Dispute Resolution" in the Missouri Bar Continuing Legal Education series. He was a founding board member of the Collaborative Family Law Association and speaks frequently to lawyers, mental health professionals, and the lay public both in Missouri and internationally. He is listed in *The Best Lawyers in America* and in *Missouri-Kansas Super Lawyers*.

Alan received a Bachelor of Music degree from Kent State University and maintains an active interest in music. He served as assistant director of the St. Louis Symphony Chorus and is the founding director of the Central Reform Congregation Choir. Reflecting another aspect of his community service, he is a past president of Kids In the Middle, an organization dedicated to helping the children of divorcing families.

Alan lives in Ladue with his wife and daughter. His other two children also live in the St. Louis area.

Alisse Camazine

Ask anyone to identify a top St. Louis divorce attorney and the name Alisse Camazine is certain to come up. Over her 30 years of legal practice, Alisse has earned the respect of lawyers, judges, and clients for her tough but fair representation of divorcing men and women. In 2007 she was named by *Missouri Lawyers Weekly* as the best divorce attorney in Missouri based on a poll of lawyers across the state.

Other recognitions of her professional excellence include receiving the Lon O. Hocker Trial Award in 1987 and being listed both as one of the top 50 women lawyers in Missouri/Kansas and as a Missouri-Kansas Super Lawyer. Alisse has been included in *The Best Lawyers in America* continuously since 1993. She is the former president of the St. Louis County Bar Association and has been a fellow of the American Academy of Matrimonial Lawyers since 1988.

Alisse has practiced in Clayton for many years and is a founding partner of Paule, Camazine & Blumenthal, P.C.

Alisse is an avid traveler and has spent time each summer over the past several years assisting at a village hospital in Nigeria that offers medical care to the poor. She also started the nonprofit Earthwide Surgical Foundation to provide medical care and education to residents of third-world nations. Alisse is a founding board member of Caring for Kids, an organization providing essential resources to meet the urgent needs of children involved with the St. Louis County Family and Truancy Courts.

Alisse, her three sons, and her husband live in Clayton.

John Pavese

As a volunteer pilot for the Chesterfield charity Wings of Hope, John travels frequently to Missouri. Over these visits one thing led to another with *Divorce in Missouri* being the final result of a three year project.

Born on Long Island, New York, John enjoyed a wide-ranging international business career before early retirement in 1998. Moving to Vermont, he followed his ambition to be both entrepreneur and freelance writer. In 2003 John coauthored the book *Divorce in Vermont*. He now lives on North Carolina's Albemarle Sound with his wife Kathy, Maple the cat, and the dog, Spanky.